Birds of New Mexico

Field Guide

by Stan Tekiela

ADVENTURE PUBLICATIONS, INC.
CAMBRIDGE, MINNESOTA

To my wife Katherine and daughter Abigail with all my love

ACKNOWLEDGMENTS

Special thanks to the National Wildlife Refuge System, which stewards the land that is critical to many bird species. Thanks also to Steve West for reviewing the range maps.

Edited by Sandy Livoti
Book design and illustrations by Jonathan Norberg
Range maps produced by Anthony Hertzel

Photo credits by photographer and page number:
Cover photo: Male Lazuli Bunting by Dudley Edmondson
Dudley Edmondson: 12, 20, 26 (perching), 36, 54, 86, 94 (female), 106, 108 (female), 140 (head), 148 (both), 158, 180 (soaring), 184 (soaring light morph), 186 (perching light morph), 188 (soaring juvenile), 230, 240 (male), 246 (female), 250, 258 (perching, soaring), 318 (winter male), 336 **B. Gerlach/DPA***: 292 (male) **Ned Harris**: 206 (juvenile) **Kevin T. Karlson**: 24, 38 (male), 178 **Bill Marchel**: 2, 82 (male), 114 (white-striped), 290 (male), 308 (female) **Steve and Dave Maslowski**: 8 (male), 64, 70, 72 (female), 102, 104, 112, 132, 200, 276 (male), 280 (male), 304, 326, 332, 338 **Anthony Mercieca/DPA***: 278 (both), 292 (female) **Steve Mortensen**: 52, 68, 168 **A. G. Nelson/DPA***: 34 **Warren Nelson**: 152 (yellow-rumped female), 324 (female) **John Pennoyer**: 88 **Johann Schumacher/CLO***: 82 (female) **Brian E. Small**: 8 (female), 32, 40 (both), 50 (winter), 76, 78, 80, 94 (Oregon female, pink-sided), 96, 98, 100, 110, 118, 120, 128, 130 (winter), 152 (red-shafted male and female), 166, 172, 196 (perching), 210 (Oregon male), 214 (Audubon's female), 216, 218, 220, 224, 234, 236 (gray morph), 248, 266, 276 (female), 280 (female), 282, 284, 294, 296, 298 (yellow male), 302, 310 (winter, juvenile), 322, 328 (all), 334 (both) **Stan Tekiela**: 4 (both), 6, 10, 14, 16, 18, 22, 26 (in flight), 28 (both), 30 (both), 38 (female), 42 (both), 44, 46, 48, 50 (breeding), 56, 58 (all), 60, 62, 66, 72 (male), 74 (both), 84, 90, 92, 108 (male), 114 (tan-striped), 116 (both), 122, 124 (adult, 1 year old), 126, 130 (breeding), 134, 136, 138, 140 (perching), 142 (all), 144, 146, 150, 152 (yellow-shafted male), 154, 156 (both), 160 (both), 162, 164, 170 (female, Mexican), 174 (both), 176, 188 (perching, soaring), 190, 192, 194 (both), 198, 202, 204, 206 (male, female), 208, 210 (male), 212, 214 (both males, Myrtle female and first winter), 222, 226, 228, 232, 238, 240 (female), 242 (both), 244 (female), 246 (male), 252, 254, 256, 258 (juvenile), 260, 264 (soaring), 268, 270 (both), 272 (all), 274 (both), 286 (male), 288, 290 (in flight), 298 (male), 300, 306, 308 (in flight), 310 (breeding, in flight), 312 (both), 314 (all), 316 (both), 318 (male, female), 320 (male), 324 (male), 330 (all) **Brian K. Wheeler**: 180 (perching), 182 (both), 184 (perching light and dark morphs, soaring dark morph, intermediate morph), 186 (perching dark morph, soaring light and dark morphs), 188 (juvenile), 196 (soaring, juvenile), 262 (all), 264 (perching) **J. R. Woodward/CLO***: 244 (displaying) **Jim Zipp**: 124 (Bohemian), 236 (brown morph), 320 (female)

*DPA: Dembinsky Photo Associates; CLO: Cornell Laboratory of Ornithology

To the best of the publisher's knowledge, all photos were of live birds.

Second Printing; Revised 2004
Published by Adventure Publications, Inc.
820 Cleveland St. S, Cambridge, MN 55008
1-800-678-7006
Printed in China

TABLE OF CONTENTS

Introduction

WHY WATCH BIRDS IN NEW MEXICO?

Millions of people have discovered bird feeding. It's a simple and enjoyable way to bring the beauty of birds closer to your home. Watching birds at your feeder often leads to a lifetime pursuit of bird identification. The *Birds of New Mexico Field Guide* is for those who want to identify the common birds of New Mexico.

There are over 800 species of birds found in North America. In New Mexico alone there have been over 300 different kinds of birds recorded throughout the years. These bird sightings were diligently recorded by hundreds of bird watchers and became part of the official state record. From these valuable records, I have chosen 143 of the most common birds of New Mexico to include in this field guide.

Bird watching, often called birding, is the largest spectator sport in America. Its outstanding popularity in New Mexico is due, in part, to an unusually rich and abundant birdlife. Why are there so many birds? One reason is open space. New Mexico is over 121,600 square miles (316,100 sq. km). Despite its size, only about 1.7 million people call New Mexico home. On average, that is only 14 people per square mile (5 per sq. km). Most of these people are located in and around only two major cities.

Open space is not the only reason there is such an abundance of birds. It's also the diversity of habitat. New Mexico can be broken into four distinct habitats–the southern extension of the Rocky Mountains, the Basin and Range, the Great Plains Province and the Colorado Plateau. Each supports a different group of birds.

Dividing the state down the middle is the southern extension of the Rocky Mountains. This section of the Rockies, which splits and runs southward along each side of the Rio Grande Valley, is a great place to see alpine birds such as the Mountain Chickadee and Gray Jay. New Mexico's most rugged mountains and highest peak–Wheeler Peak–are found in this area.

The Basin and Range is New Mexico's largest province. It extends down the middle of the state between the two extensions of the

Rocky Mountains and southwest and south central New Mexico. It is a broad, dry region that drains the surrounding mountains. The largest basins are the Estancia and Tularosa. This province is a good place to see the Gambel's Quail and Pyrrhuloxia.

To the east of the Rocky Mountains lies the Great Plains Province, which runs north to south and is 100-150 miles (160-240 km) wide. The habitat is mainly dry, sparsely vegetated high plains, but it is home to many great birds such as the Common Raven and Golden Eagle.

West of the Rockies is a relatively flat terrain called the Colorado Plateau. A thinly populated region, it's one of the most beautiful. An arid place from 5,000-7,000 feet (1,500-2,150 m), most of this area consists of brightly colored sandstone. Open country birds such as Red-tailed and Ferruginous Hawks live here.

Water also plays a big part in the state's bird populations. There are more than 230 square miles (600 sq. km) of water surface in New Mexico. From the Rio Grande to the Pecos and San Juan Rivers, and from Elephant Butte Reservoir to Caballo Reservoir, this essential element supports a wide variety of water-loving birds such as Red-winged Blackbirds and American Avocets.

Varying habitats in New Mexico also mean variations in weather. Since elevation rises from nearly 2,850 feet (850 m) in eastern plains to over 13,000 feet (3,950 m) at mountaintops, there are great differences in weather. Tall peaks such as North Truchas Peak are some of the coldest, snowiest places, while the Great Plains flatlands are the beneficiary of warming air as it moves down from the high country. The Rockies in central New Mexico create a moisture barrier, which results in a rain shadow effect in the eastern part of the state, making it much drier there.

No matter if you are in the hot, dry Great Plains Province or in the cool, moist Rocky Mountains, there are birds to watch in each season. Whether witnessing a migration of hawks in the fall or welcoming back hummingbirds in spring, there is variety and excitement in birding as each season turns to the next.

OBSERVE WITH A STRATEGY;
TIPS FOR IDENTIFYING BIRDS

Identifying birds isn't as difficult as you might think. By simply following a few basic strategies, you can increase your chances of successfully identifying most birds you see! One of the first and easiest things to do when you see a new bird is to note its color. (Also, since this book is organized by color, you will go right to that color section to find it.)

Next, note the size of the bird. A strategy to quickly estimate size is to select a small-, medium- and large-sized bird to use for reference. For example, most people are familiar with robins. A robin, measured from tip of the bill to tip of the tail, is 10 inches (25 cm) long. Using the robin as an example of a medium-sized bird, select two other birds, one smaller and one larger. Many people use a House Sparrow, at about 6 inches (15 cm), and an American Crow, about 18 inches (45 cm). When you see a bird that you don't know, you can quickly ask yourself, "Is it smaller than a robin, but larger than a sparrow?" When you look in your field guide to help identify your bird, you'll know it's roughly between 6-10 inches (15-25 cm) long. This will help to narrow your choices.

Next, note the size, shape and color of the bill. Is it long, short, thick, thin, pointed, blunt, curved or straight? Seed-eating birds such as Evening Grosbeaks have bills that are thick and strong enough to crack even the toughest seeds. Birds that sip nectar such as Black-chinned Hummingbirds need long thin bills to reach deep into flowers. Hawks and owls tear their prey with very sharp, curving bills. Sometimes, just noting the bill shape can help you decide if the bird is a woodpecker, finch, grosbeak, blackbird or bird of prey.

Next, take a look around and note the habitat in which you see the bird. Is it wading in a marsh? Walking along a riverbank? Soaring in the sky? Is it perched high in the trees or hopping along the forest floor? Because of their preferences in diet and habitat, you'll usually see robins hopping on the ground, but not often eating the seeds at your feeder. Or you'll see a Black-headed Grosbeak sitting on a branch of a tree, but not climbing down the tree trunk headfirst the way a nuthatch does.

Noticing what a bird is eating will give you another clue to help you identify that bird. Feeding is a big part of any bird's life. Fully one-third of all bird activity revolves around searching for and catching food, or actually eating. While birds don't always follow all the rules of what we think they eat, you can make some general assumptions. Northern Flickers, for instance, feed upon ants and other insects, so you wouldn't expect to see them visiting a backyard feeder. Some birds such as Barn Swallows and Cliff Swallows feed upon flying insects and spend hours swooping and diving to catch a meal.

Sometimes you can identify a bird by the way it perches. Body posture can help you differentiate between an American Crow and a Red-tailed Hawk. American Crows lean forward over their feet on a branch, while hawks perch in a vertical position. Look for this the next time you see a large unidentified bird in a tree.

Birds in flight are often difficult to identify, but noting the size and shape of the wing will help. A bird's wing size is in direct proportion to its body size, weight and type of flying. The shape of the wing determines if the bird flies fast and with precision, or slowly and less precisely. Birds such as House Finches, which flit around in thick tangles of branches, have short round wings. Birds that soar on warm updrafts of air, such as Turkey Vultures, have long broad wings. Barn Swallows have short pointed wings that slice through air, propelling their swift and accurate flight.

Some birds have unique flight patterns that aid in identification. American Goldfinches fly in a distinctive up-and-down pattern that makes it look as if they are riding a roller coaster.

While it's not easy to make these observations in the short time you often have to watch a "mystery bird," practicing these methods of identification will greatly expand your skills in birding. Also, seek the guidance of a more experienced birder who will help you improve your skills and answer questions on the spot.

BIRD BASICS

It's easier to identify birds and communicate about them if you know the names of the different parts of a bird. For instance, it's more effective to use the word "crest" to indicate the set of extra long feathers on top of the head of a Steller's Jay than to try to describe it.

The following illustration points out the basic parts of a bird. Because it is a composite of many birds, it shouldn't be confused with any actual bird.

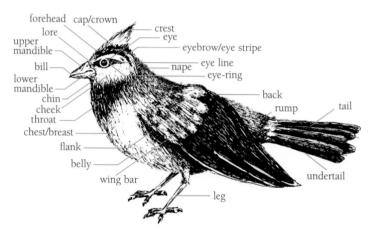

BIRD COLOR VARIABLES

No other animal has a color pallet like a bird's. Brilliant blues, lemon yellows, showy reds and iridescent greens are commonplace within the bird world. In general, the male birds are more colorful than their female counterparts. This is probably to help the male attract a mate, essentially saying, "Hey, look at me!" It also calls attention to the male's overall health. The better the condition of his feathers, the better his food source and territory, and therefore the better his potential for a mate.

Female birds that don't look like their male counterparts (such species are called sexually dimorphic, meaning "two forms") are often a nondescript color, as seen with the Lazuli Bunting. These muted tones help hide the females during weeks of motionless incubation, and draw less attention to them when they are out feeding or taking a break from the rigors of raising their young.

In some species such as the Bald Eagle, Steller's Jay and Downy Woodpecker, the male birds look nearly identical to the females. In the case of the woodpeckers, the sexes are only differentiated by a single red or sometimes yellow mark. Depending on the species, the mark may be on top of the head, face, nape of the neck or just behind the bill.

During the first year, juvenile birds often look like the mothers. Since brightly colored feathers are used mainly for attracting a mate, young non-breeding males don't have a need for colorful plumage. It is not until the first spring molt (or several years later, depending on the species) that young males obtain their breeding colors.

Both breeding and winter plumages are the result of molting. Molting is the process of dropping old worn feathers and replacing them with new ones. All birds molt, typically twice a year, with the spring molt usually occurring in late winter. During this time, most birds produce their breeding plumage (brighter colors for attracting mates), which lasts throughout the summer.

Winter plumage is the result of the late summer molt, which serves a couple of important functions. First, it adds feathers for warmth in the coming winter. Second, in some species it produces feathers that tend to be drab in color, which helps to camouflage the birds and hide them from predators. The winter plumage of the male American Goldfinch, for example, is an olive brown unlike its obvious canary yellow color in summer. Luckily for us, some birds such as Lewis's Woodpeckers retain their bright summer colors all year long.

BIRD NESTS

Bird nests are truly an amazing feat of engineering. Imagine building your home strong enough to weather a storm, large enough to hold your entire family, insulated enough to shelter them from cold and heat, and waterproof enough to keep out rain. Now, build it without any blueprints or directions, and without the use of your hands or feet! Birds do!

Before building a nest, an appropriate site must be selected. In some species such as House Wrens, the male picks out several potential sites and assembles several small twigs in each. This discourages other birds from using nearby nest cavities. These "extra" nests are occasionally called dummy nests. The female is then taken around and shown all the choices. She chooses her favorite and finishes constructing the nest. In some other species of birds–the Bullock's Oriole, for example–it is the female who chooses the site and builds the nest with the male offering only an occasional suggestion. Each species has its own nest-building routine, which is strictly followed.

Nesting material usually consists of natural elements found in the immediate area. Most nests consist of plant fibers (such as bark peeled from grapevines), sticks, mud, dried grass, feathers, fur, or soft fuzzy tufts from thistle. Some birds, including Broad-tailed Hummingbirds, use spider webs to glue nesting materials together. Nesting material is limited to what a bird can hold or carry. Because of this, a bird must make many trips afield to gather enough materials to complete its nest. Most nests take at least four days or more, and hundreds, if not thousands, of trips to build.

As you'll see in the following illustrations, birds build a wide variety of nest types.

ground nest   platform nest   cup nest   pendulous nest

The simple **ground nest** is scraped out of the earth. A shallow depression that usually contains no nesting material, it is made by birds such as the Killdeer and Horned Lark.

Another kind of nest, the **platform nest**, represents a more complex type of nest building. Constructed of small twigs and branches, the platform nest is a simple arrangement of sticks which forms a platform and features a small depression to nestle the eggs.

Some platform nests, such as those of the Canada Goose, are constructed on the ground and are made with mud and grass. Platform nests can also be on cliffs, bridges, balconies or even in flowerpots. This kind of nest gives space to adventurous youngsters and functions as a landing platform for the parents. Many waterfowl construct platform nests on the ground, usually near water or actually in the water. These floating platform nests vary with the water level, thus preventing nests with eggs from being flooded. Platform nests, constructed by such birds as Mourning Doves and herons, are not anchored to the tree and may tumble from the branches during high winds and storms.

The **cup nest** is a modified platform nest, used by three-quarters of all songbirds. Constructed from the outside in, a supporting platform is constructed first. This platform is attached firmly to a tree, shrub, rock ledge or the ground. Next, the sides are constructed of grasses, small twigs, bark or leaves, which are woven together and often glued with mud for additional strength. The inner cup, lined with feathers, animal fur, soft plant material or animal hair, is constructed last. The mother bird uses her chest to cast the final contours of the inner nest.

The **pendulous nest** is an unusual nest, looking more like a sock hanging from a branch than a nest. Inaccessible to most predators, these nests are attached to the ends of the smallest branches of a tree, and often wave wildly in the breeze. Woven very tightly of plant fibers, they are strong and watertight, taking up to a week to build. More commonly used by tropical birds, this complicated nest type has also been mastered by orioles and kinglets. A small opening on the top or side allows the parents access to the grass-lined interior. (It must be one heck of a ride to be inside one of these nests during a windy spring thunderstorm!)

One of the most clever of all nest types is known as the **no nest** or daycare nest. Parasitic birds such as Brown-headed Cowbirds build no nests at all! The egg-laden female expertly searches out other birds' nests and sneaks in to lay one of her own eggs while the host mother is not looking, thereby leaving the host mother to raise an adopted youngster. The mother cowbird wastes no energy building a nest only to have it raided by a predator. By using several nests of other birds, she spreads out her progeny so at least one of her offspring will live to maturity.

Another type of nest, the **cavity nest**, is used by many birds, including woodpeckers and Western Bluebirds. The cavity nest is usually excavated in a tree branch or trunk and offers shelter from storms, sun, predators and cold. A relatively small entrance hole in a tree leads to an inner chamber up to 10 inches (25 cm) below. Usually constructed by woodpeckers, the cavity nest is typically used only once by its builder, but subsequently can be used for many years by birds such as mergansers, Tree Swallows and bluebirds, which do not have the capability of excavating one for themselves. Kingfishers, on the other hand, excavate a tunnel up to 4 feet (1 m) long, which connects the entrance in a riverbank to the nest chamber. These cavity nests are often sparsely lined because they are already well insulated.

Some birds, including some swallows, take nest building one step further. They use a collection of small balls of mud to construct an adobe-style home. Constructed beneath the eaves of houses, under bridges or inside chimneys, some of these nests look like simple cup nests. Others are completely enclosed, with small tunnel-like openings that lead into a safe nesting chamber for the baby birds.

WHO BUILDS THE NEST?

In general, the female bird builds the nest. She gathers nesting materials and constructs a nest, with an occasional visit from her mate to check on the progress. In some species, both parents contribute equally to the construction of a nest. A male bird might forage for precisely the right sticks, grass or mud, but it's often the female that forms or puts together the nest. She uses her body to form the egg chamber. Rarely does the male build a nest by himself.

FLEDGING

Fledging is the interval between hatching and flight or leaving the nest. Some birds leave the nest within hours of hatching (precocial), but it might be weeks before they are able to fly. This is common with waterfowl and shorebirds. Until they start to fly, they are called fledglings. Birds that are still in the nest are called nestlings. Other baby birds are born naked and blind, and remain in the nest for several weeks (altricial).

WHY BIRDS MIGRATE

Why do birds migrate? The short answer is simple–food. Birds migrate to areas with high concentrations of food, as it is easier to breed where food is than where it is not. A typical migrating bird–the Western Tanager, for instance–will migrate from the tropics of Central America and Mexico to nest in forests of North America, taking advantage of billions of newly hatched insects to feed its young. This trip is called **complete migration**.

Some birds of prey return from their complete migration to northern regions that are overflowing with small rodents such as mice and voles that have continued to breed in winter.

Complete migrators have a set time and pattern of migration. Each year at nearly the same time, they take off and head for a specific wintering ground. Complete migrators may travel great distances, sometimes as much as 15,000 miles (24,150 km) or more in a year. But complete migration doesn't necessarily imply flying from the cold, frozen northland to a tropical destination. The Swainson's Hawk, for example, is a complete migrator that flies from New Mexico to spend the winter in Central and South America. This is still called complete migration.

There are many interesting aspects to complete migrators. In the spring, males usually migrate several weeks before the females, arriving early to scope out possibilities for nesting sites and food sources, and to begin to defend territories. The females arrive several weeks later. In the autumn, in many species, the females and their young leave early, often up to four weeks before the adult males.

All migrators are not the same type. There are **partial migrators** such as American Goldfinches that usually wait until the food supply dwindles before flying south. Unlike complete migrators, the partial migrators move only far enough south, or sometimes east and west, to find abundant food. In some years it might be only a few hundred miles, while in other years it might be nearly a thousand. This kind of migration, dependent on the weather and available food, is sometimes called **seasonal movement**.

Unlike the predictable ebbing and flowing behavior of complete migrators or partial migrators, **irruptive migrators** can move every third to fifth year or, in some cases, in consecutive years. These migrations are triggered when times are really tough and food is scarce. Red-breasted Nuthatches are a good example of irruptive migrators, because they leave their normal northern range in search of food or in response to overpopulation.

HOW DO BIRDS MIGRATE?

One of the many secrets of migration is fat. While we humans are fighting the battle of the bulge, birds intentionally gorge themselves to put on as much fat as possible while still being able to fly. Fat provides the greatest amount of energy per unit of weight, and in the same way that your car needs gas, birds are propelled by fat and stalled without it.

During long migratory flights, fat deposits are used up quickly, and birds need to stop to "refuel." This is when backyard bird feeding stations and undeveloped, natural spaces around our towns and cities are especially important. Some birds require up to 2-3 days of constant feeding to build their fat reserves before continuing their seasonal trip.

Some birds such as most eagles, hawks, falcons and vultures migrate during the day. Larger birds can hold more body fat, go longer without eating and take longer to migrate. These birds glide on rising columns of warm air, called thermals, which hold them aloft while they slowly make their way north or south. They generally rest during nights and hunt early in the morning before the sun has a chance to warm up the land and create good soaring conditions. Birds migrating during the day use a combination of landforms, rivers, and the rising and setting sun to guide them in the right direction.

Most other birds migrate during the night. Studies show that some birds which migrate at night use the stars to navigate. Others use the setting sun, while still others such as doves use the earth's magnetic fields to guide them north or south. While flying at night might seem like a crazy idea, nocturnal migration is safer for several reasons. First, there are fewer nighttime predators for migrating birds. Second, traveling at night allows time during the day to find food in unfamiliar surroundings. Finally, nighttime wind patterns tend to be flat, or laminar. These flat winds don't have the turbulence associated with the daytime winds and can actually help carry smaller birds by pushing them along.

HOW TO USE THIS GUIDE

To help you quickly and easily identify birds, this book is organized by color. Simply note the color of the bird and turn to that section. Refer to the first page for the color key. The Red-naped Sapsucker, for example, is black and white with red on its head. Because the bird is mostly black and white, it will be found in the black and white section. Each color section is also arranged by size, generally with smaller birds first. Sections may also incorporate the average size in a range, which, in some cases, reflects size differences between male and female birds. Flip through the pages in that color section to find the bird. If you already know the name of the bird, check the index for the page number. In some species, the male and female are remarkably different in color. In these cases, the opposite sex is shown in a smaller inset photograph with a page reference. These birds, therefore, will be found in two different color sections.

In the description section you will find a variety of information about the bird. On page 1 is a sample of the information that is included in the book.

RANGE MAPS

Range maps are included for each bird. Colored areas indicate where in the state a particular bird is most likely to be found. Green is used for summer, blue for winter, red for year-round and yellow for areas where the bird is seen during migration. While every effort has been made to accurately depict these ranges, they are only general guidelines. Ranges actually change on an ongoing basis due to a variety of factors. Changes in weather, species abundance, landscape and vital resources such as the availability of food and water can affect local populations, migration and movements, causing birds to be found in areas that are atypical for the species.

Colored areas simply mean bird sightings for that species have been frequent in those areas and less frequent in the others. Please use the maps as intended–as general guides only.

COMMON NAME
Scientific name

YEAR-ROUND
MIGRATION
SUMMER
WINTER

Size: measures head to tail, may include wingspan

Male: a brief description of the male bird, and may include breeding, winter or other plumages

Female: a brief description of the female bird, which is sometimes not the same as the male

Juvenile: a brief description of the juvenile bird, which often looks like the female

Nest: the kind of nest this bird builds to raise its young; who builds the nest; how many broods per year

Eggs: how many eggs you might expect to see in a nest; color and marking

Incubation: the average time parents spend incubating the eggs; who does the incubation

Fledging: the average time young spend in the nest after hatching but before they leave the nest; who does the most "childcare" and feeding

Migration: complete (consistent, seasonal), partial migrator (seasonal, destination varies), irruptive (unpredictable, depends on the food supply), non-migrator; additional comments

Food: what the bird eats most of the time (e.g., seeds, insects, fruit, nectar, small mammals, fish); if it typically comes to a bird feeding station

Compare: notes about other birds that look similar, and the pages on which they can be found

Stan's Notes: Interesting gee-whiz natural history information. This could be something to look or listen for, or something to help positively identify the bird. Also includes remarkable features.

female pg. 127

male

BROWN-HEADED COWBIRD
Molothrus ater

Size: 7½" (19 cm)

Male: A glossy black bird, reminiscent of a Red-winged Blackbird. Chocolate brown head with a pointed, sharp gray bill.

Female: dull brown bird with bill similar to male

Juvenile: similar to female, only dull gray color and a streaked chest

Nest: no nest; lays eggs in nests of other birds

Eggs: 5-7; white with brown markings

Incubation: 10-13 days; host bird incubates eggs

Fledging: 10-11 days; host birds feed young

Migration: non-migrator to partial in New Mexico

Food: insects, seeds; will come to seed feeders

Compare: The male Red-winged Blackbird (pg. 11) is slightly larger, with red and yellow patches on upper wings. Common Grackle (pg. 17) has a long tail and lacks the brown head. European Starling (pg. 5) has a shorter tail.

Stan's Notes: A member of the blackbird family. Of approximately 750 species of parasitic birds worldwide, this is the only parasitic bird in the state, laying eggs in host birds' nests, leaving others to raise its young. Cowbirds are known to have laid eggs in nests of over 200 species of birds. Some birds reject cowbird eggs, but most incubate them and raise the young, even to the exclusion of their own. Look for warblers and other birds feeding young birds twice their own size. At one time cowbirds followed bison to feed on insects attracted to the animals.

winter

breeding

EUROPEAN STARLING
Sturnus vulgaris

Size: 7½" (19 cm)

Male: Gray-to-black bird with white speckles in fall and winter. Shiny purple black during spring and summer. Long, pointed yellow bill in spring turns gray in fall. Short tail.

Female: same as male

Juvenile: similar to adult, gray brown in color with a streaked chest

Nest: cavity; male and female line the cavity; 2 broods per year

Eggs: 4-6; bluish with brown markings

Incubation: 12-14 days; female and male incubate

Fledging: 18-20 days; female and male feed young

Migration: non-migrator

Food: insects, seeds, fruit; comes to seed and suet feeders

Compare: Similar to Common Grackle (pg. 17), but lacks its long tail. The male Brown-headed Cowbird (pg. 3) is the same size, but has a brown head and longer tail.

Stan's Notes: A great songster, this bird can mimic other birds and sounds. Often displaces woodpeckers, chickadees and other cavity-nesting birds. Can be very aggressive and destroy eggs or young of other birds. Bill changes color with the seasons: yellow in spring, gray in autumn. Jaws are designed to be the most powerful when opening, as they pry open crevices to locate hidden insects. Gathers in the hundreds in autumn. Not a native bird, it was introduced to New York City in 1890-91 from Europe.

male

female
pg. 229

PHAINOPEPLA
Phainopepla nitens

Size: 8" (20 cm)

Male: Slim, long, glossy black bird with a ragged crest and deep red eyes. Wing patches near tips of wings are white, obvious in flight.

Female: slim, long, mostly gray bird with a ragged crest and deep red eyes, whitish wing bars

Juvenile: similar to female

Nest: cup; female and male construct; 1-2 broods per year

Eggs: 2-4; gray with brown markings

Incubation: 12-14 days; female and male incubate

Fledging: 18-20 days; female and male feed young

Migration: complete, to Arizona and California

Food: fruit (usually mistletoe), insects; will come to water elements or water drips in yards

Compare: The only all-black bird with a crest and red eyes. Look for white wing patches in flight.

Stan's Notes: Seen in desert scrub with water and mistletoe nearby. Gives a low, liquid "kweer" song, but will also mimic other species. In winter individuals defend food supply such as a single tree with abundant mistletoe berries. Probably responsible for the dispersal of mistletoe plants far and wide. Male will fly up to a height of 300 feet (90 m), circling and zigzagging to court female. Builds nest of twigs and plant fibers and binds it with spider webs in the crotch of a mistletoe cluster. Lines nest with hair or soft plant fibers. May be the only species to nest in two regions in the same nest season. Nests in dry desert habitat in early spring. When it gets hot, moves to a higher area with an abundant water supply to nest again.

male

female

SPOTTED TOWHEE
Pipilo maculatus

YEAR-ROUND
MIGRATION

Size: 8½" (22 cm)

Male: A mostly black bird with dirty red-brown sides and white belly. Multiple white spots on wings and sides. Long black tail with a white tip. Rich red eyes.

Female: very similar to male, with a brown head

Juvenile: brown with a heavily streaked chest

Nest: cup; female builds; 1-2 broods per year

Eggs: 3-5; white with brown markings

Incubation: 12-14 days; female and male incubate

Fledging: 10-12 days; female and male feed young

Migration: non-migrator to partial migrator

Food: seeds, fruit, insects

Compare: Closely related to the Green-tailed Towhee (pg. 283), which appears nothing like the bold black and red of the Spotted Towhee.

Stan's Notes: Not as common as the Green-tailed Towhee, but it inhabits a similar habitat. Found in a variety of habitats, from thick brush and chaparral to suburban backyards. Often heard noisily scratching through dead leaves on the ground for food. More than 70 percent of its diet is plant material. Eats more insects in spring and summer. Well known for retreating from danger by walking away rather than taking to flight. Cup nest is nearly always on the ground under bushes, but away from where male perches to sing. Begins breeding in April. Lays eggs in May. After breeding season, moves to higher elevations. Song and plumage vary geographically and are not well studied or understood.

female pg. 137

male

RED-WINGED BLACKBIRD
Agelaius phoeniceus

Size: 8½" (22 cm)

Male: Jet black bird with red and yellow shoulder patches on upper wings. Pointed black bill.

Female: heavily streaked brown bird with a pointed brown bill and white eyebrows

Juvenile: same as female

Nest: cup; female builds; 2-3 broods per year

Eggs: 3-4; bluish green with brown markings

Incubation: 10-12 days; female incubates

Fledging: 11-14 days; female and male feed young

Migration: non-migrator to partial migrator

Food: seeds, insects; will come to seed feeders

Compare: Slightly larger than the male Brown-headed Cowbird (pg. 3), but is less iridescent and lacks the Cowbird's brown head. Differs from all other blackbirds due to the red and yellow patches on its wings (epaulets).

Stan's Notes: One of the most widespread and numerous birds in the state. It is a sure sign of spring when the Red-winged Blackbirds return to the marshes. Flocks of up to 100,000 birds have been reported. Males return before the females and defend territories by singing from tops of surrounding vegetation. Males repeat call from the tops of cattails while showing off their red and yellow wing bars (epaulets). Females choose mate and usually will nest over shallow water in thick stands of cattails. Red-wingeds feed mostly on seeds in fall and spring, switching to insects during summer.

11

female pg. 139

male

BREWER'S BLACKBIRD
Euphagus cyanocephalus

YEAR-ROUND
WINTER

Size: 9" (22.5 cm)

Male: Overall glossy black, shining green in direct light. Head more purple than green. Bright white or pale yellow eyes. Winter plumage can be dull gray to black.

Female: similar to male, only overall grayish brown, most have dark eyes

Juvenile: similar to female

Nest: cup; female builds; 1-2 broods per year

Eggs: 4-6; gray with brown markings

Incubation: 12-14 days; female incubates

Fledging: 13-14 days; female and male feed young

Migration: non-migrator to partial in New Mexico

Food: insects, seeds, fruit

Compare: Smaller than the Common Grackle (pg. 17) and the male Great-tailed Grackle (pg. 21), lacking their long tails. Male Brown-headed Cowbird (pg. 3) is smaller and has a brown head. Male Red-winged Blackbird (pg. 11) has red and yellow shoulder marks.

Stan's Notes: Often in fields and open places such as wet pastures and mountain meadows up to 10,000 feet (3,050 m). Male and some females are easily identified by their bright, nearly white eyes. A cowbird host. Usually nests in a shrub, small tree or on ground. Prefers to nest in small colonies, up to 20 pairs. Doesn't get along with Common Grackles; often driven out of nest area by expansion of grackles. Gathers in large flocks with cowbirds, Red-wingeds and other blackbirds to migrate. Expanding its range in North America.

13

female
pg. 147

male

MIGRATION
SUMMER
WINTER

YELLOW-HEADED BLACKBIRD
Xanthocephalus xanthocephalus

Size: 9-11" (22.5-28 cm)

Male: Large black bird with a lemon yellow head, chest and nape of neck. Black mask and a gray bill. White wing patches.

Female: similar to male, only slightly smaller with a brown body, dull yellow head and chest

Juvenile: similar to female

Nest: cup; female builds; 2 broods per year

Eggs: 3-5; greenish white with brown markings

Incubation: 11-13 days; female incubates

Fledging: 9-12 days; female feeds young

Migration: complete, to southern New Mexico, Mexico

Food: insects, seeds; will come to ground feeders

Compare: Larger than the male Red-winged Blackbird (pg. 11), which has red and yellow patches on its wings. Male Yellow-headed Blackbird is the only large black bird with a bright yellow head.

Stan's Notes: Usually heard before seen, Yellow-headed Blackbird has a low, hoarse, raspy or metallic call. Nests in deep water marshes unlike its cousin, the Red-winged Blackbird, which prefers shallow water. The male gives an impressive mating display, flying with head drooped and feet and tail pointing down while steadily beating its wings. The female incubates alone and feeds 3-5 young. Young keep low and out of sight for as many as three weeks before starting to fly. Migrates in flocks of up to 200 with other blackbirds. Flocks made up mainly of males return first in early April; females return later. Most colonies consist of 20-100 nests.

YEAR-ROUND
SUMMER

COMMON GRACKLE
Quiscalus quiscula

Size: 11-13" (28-33 cm)

Male: Large black bird with iridescent blue black head, purple brown body, long black tail, long thin bill and bright golden eyes.

Female: similar to male, only duller and smaller

Juvenile: similar to female

Nest: cup; female builds; 2 broods per year

Eggs: 4-5; greenish white with brown markings

Incubation: 13-14 days; female incubates

Fledging: 16-20 days; female and male feed young

Migration: complete to partial migrator; moves around to find food

Food: fruit, seeds, insects; comes to seed feeders

Compare: Male Great-tailed Grackle (pg. 21) is larger than the Common Grackle and has a much longer tail. The European Starling (pg. 5) is much smaller with a speckled appearance, and yellow bill during the breeding season. Male Red-winged Blackbird (pg. 11) has red and yellow wing markings.

Stan's Notes: Usually nests in small colonies of up to 75 pairs, but travels with other blackbirds in large flocks. Is known to feed in farmers' fields. The name is derived from the Latin word *graculus*, meaning "to cough," for its loud raspy call. Holds tail in a vertical keel-like position during flight. The flight pattern is almost always level, as opposed to an undulating up-and-down movement. Unlike most birds, it has larger muscles for opening the mouth (rather than for closing it) and prying crevices apart to locate hidden insects.

AMERICAN COOT
Fulica americana

YEAR-ROUND

Size: 13-16" (33-40 cm)

Male: Slate gray to black all over, white bill with dark band near tip. Green legs and feet. A small white patch near the base of the tail. Prominent red eyes, with a small red patch above bill between eyes.

Female: same as male

Juvenile: much paler than adult, with a gray bill and same white rump patch

Nest: floating platform; female and male build; 1 brood per year

Eggs: 9-12; pinkish buff with brown markings

Incubation: 21-25 days; female and male incubate

Fledging: 49-52 days; female and male feed young

Migration: non-migrator to partial in New Mexico

Food: insects, aquatic plants

Compare: Smaller than most waterfowl, it is the only black water bird or duck-like bird with a white bill.

Stan's Notes: An excellent diver and swimmer, often seen in large flocks on open water. Not a duck, as it doesn't have webbed feet, but instead has large lobed toes. When taking off, scrambles across surface of water with wings flapping. Bobs head while swimming. Nest is a floating mat of vegetation. Huge flocks of as many as 1,000 birds gather for migration and during winter. The unusual name is of unknown origin, but in Middle English, *coote* was used to describe various waterfowl–perhaps it stuck. Also called Mud Hen.

female pg. 159

male

GREAT-TAILED GRACKLE
Quiscalus mexicanus

Size: 18" (45 cm), male
15" (38 cm), female

Male: A large all-black bird with iridescent purple sheen on the head and back. Exceptionally long tail. Bright yellow eyes.

Female: considerably smaller than the male, overall brown bird with gray-to-brown belly, light brown-to-white eyes, eyebrows, throat and upper chest

Juvenile: similar to female

Nest: cup; female builds; 1-2 broods per year

Eggs: 3-5; greenish blue with brown markings

Incubation: 12-14 days; female incubates

Fledging: 21-23 days; female feeds young

Migration: non-migrator to partial in New Mexico; will move around to find food

Food: insects, fruit, seeds; comes to seed feeders

Compare: Common Grackle (pg. 17) is smaller, with a much shorter tail.

Stan's Notes: This is our largest grackle. It was once considered a subspecies of the Boat-tailed Grackle, which occurs along the East coast and Florida. A bird that prefers to nest near water in an open habitat. A colony nester, males do not participate in nest building, incubation or raising of young. Males rarely fight, but females will squabble over nest sites and materials. Several females mate with one male. They are expanding northward, moving into northern states. Western populations tend to be larger than the eastern. Song varies from population to population.

AMERICAN CROW
Corvus brachyrhynchos

YEAR-ROUND

Size: 18" (45 cm)

Male: All-black bird with black bill, legs and feet. Can have a purple sheen in direct sunlight.

Female: same as male

Juvenile: same as adult

Nest: platform; female builds; 1 brood per year

Eggs: 4-6; bluish to olive green, brown markings

Incubation: 18 days; female incubates

Fledging: 28-35 days; female and male feed young

Migration: non-migrator to partial migrator

Food: fruit, insects, mammals, fish, carrion; will come to seed and suet feeders

Compare: Similar to Chihuahuan Raven (pg. 25) and Common Raven (pg. 27), but has a smaller bill and lacks shaggy throat feathers. Crow's call is higher than the Raven's raspy, low call. Crow has a squared tail. The Raven has a wedge-shaped tail, apparent during flight. Black-billed Magpie (pg. 55) has a long tail.

Stan's Notes: One of the most recognizable birds in New Mexico. More common than its cousin, the raven. Often reuses nest every year if not taken over by a Great Horned Owl. Collects and stores bright, shiny objects in nest. Able to mimic other birds and human voices. It is one of the smartest of all birds and very social, often entertaining itself by provoking chases with other birds. Feeds on road kill but is rarely hit by cars. Can live up to 20 years. Unmated birds known as helpers help raise young. Large extended families roost together at night, dispersing during the day to hunt.

YEAR-ROUND

CHIHUAHUAN RAVEN
Corvus cryptoleucus

Size: 20" (50 cm)

Male: A large all-black bird with a large black bill. Long bristle-like feathers cover more than half the length of the bill. Slightly shaggy throat feathers. Black legs and feet.

Female: same as male

Juvenile: similar to adult, but color of feathers on the neck is sometimes lighter

Nest: cup; female builds; 1 brood per year

Eggs: 5-7; gray to green with brown markings

Incubation: 19-21 days; female and male incubate

Fledging: 28-30 days; female and male feed young

Migration: partial migrator to non-migrator, to Mexico

Food: seeds, leaves, insects, fruit, small mammals

Compare: Common Raven (pg. 27) is very similar, but larger and has a lower-pitched call. The American Crow (pg. 23) lacks the shaggy throat and has a similar call, but it is lower in pitch than the Chihuahuan Raven's call.

Stan's Notes: Often confused with crows and other ravens. Usually found in open flat regions. Known to cache food. Male performs an impressive aerial display, soaring and tumbling, then standing in front of female with neck feathers fluffed. Builds a loose cup nest of sticks and lines it with hair and dry grass. Nest is usually solitary in a tree. Will reuse its nest several years in a row. Often breeds late in the season, presumably to time hatching with the flush of insects after the rainy season. Forms large flocks of up to several hundred after young leave the nest and throughout the winter.

in flight

COMMON RAVEN
Corvus corax

YEAR-ROUND
WINTER

Size: 22-27" (56-69 cm)

Male: Large all-black bird with a large black bill, a shaggy beard of feathers on the chin and throat, and a large wedge-shaped tail, seen in flight.

Female: same as male

Juvenile: same as adult

Nest: platform; female and male build; 1 brood per year

Eggs: 4-6; pale green with brown markings

Incubation: 18-21 days; female incubates

Fledging: 38-44 days; female and male feed young

Migration: non-migrator to partial migrator; will move around to find food

Food: insects, fruit, small animals, carrion

Compare: Very similar to but larger than Chihuahuan Raven (pg. 25). American Crow (pg. 23) is smaller and lacks the shaggy throat feathers. A low, raspy call compared with the higher-pitched call of the Chihuahuan Raven and Crow. Glides on flat, outstretched wings unlike the slight V-shaped pattern of Crow.

Stan's Notes: Considered by some to be the smartest of all birds. Known for its aerial acrobatics and long swooping dives. Scavenges with crows and gulls. Known to follow wolf packs around to pick up scraps and pick at bones of a kill. Complex courtship includes grabbing bills, preening each other and cooing. Most begin to breed at 3-4 years. Mates for life. Uses same nest site for many years.

soaring

TURKEY VULTURE
Cathartes aura

Size: 26-32" (66-80 cm); up to 6-foot wingspan

Male: Large bird with obvious red head and legs. In flight, the wings appear two-toned: black leading edge with gray on the trailing edge and tip. The tips of wings end in finger-like projections. Long squared tail. Ivory bill.

Female: same as male

Juvenile: similar to adult, with gray-to-blackish head and bill

Nest: no nest, or minimal nest on cliff or in cave; 1 brood per year

Eggs: 2; white with brown markings

Incubation: 38-41 days; female and male incubate

Fledging: 66-88 days; female and male feed young

Migration: complete, to Mexico, Central America and South America

Food: carrion; parents regurgitate for young

Compare: Smaller than the Bald Eagle (pg. 59), look for Turkey Vulture's two-toned wings. Flies holding wings in a slight V shape unlike the Bald Eagle's straight wing position.

Stan's Notes: The vulture's naked head is an adaptation to reduce risk of feather fouling (picking up diseases) from carcasses. Unlike hawks and eagles, it has weak feet more suited to walking than grasping. One of the few birds that has a developed sense of smell. Mostly mute, making only grunts and groans. Seen in trees with wings outstretched to catch sun. Recent studies show this bird is closely related to storks, not birds of prey.

29

male

female

DOWNY WOODPECKER
Picoides pubescens

YEAR-ROUND
MIGRATION

Size: 6" (15 cm)

Male: A small woodpecker with an all-white belly, black-and-white spotted wings, a black line running through the eyes, a short black bill, a white stripe down the back and red mark on the back of the head. Several small black spots along the sides of white tail.

Female: same as male, but lacks a red mark on head

Juvenile: same as female, some have a red mark near the forehead

Nest: cavity; male and female excavate; 1 brood per year

Eggs: 3-5; white without markings

Incubation: 11-12 days; female and male incubate, the female incubates during day, male at night

Fledging: 20-25 days; male and female feed young

Migration: non-migrator

Food: insects, seeds; visits seed and suet feeders

Compare: Almost identical to the Hairy Woodpecker (pg. 43), but smaller. Look for the shorter, thinner bill of Downy to differentiate them.

Stan's Notes: Abundant and widespread where trees are present. Stiff tail feathers help brace it like a tripod as it clings to a tree. Like all woodpeckers, it has a long barbed tongue to pull insects from tiny places. Male and female will drum on branches or hollow logs to announce territories, which are rarely larger than 5 acres (2 ha). Male performs most brooding. Will winter roost in cavity. Doesn't breed in high elevations, but often moves there in winter for food.

31

PAINTED REDSTART
Myioborus pictus

SUMMER

Size: 6" (15 cm)

Male: Nearly all-black bird with a white patch on the wings and white outer tail feathers. A crescent-shaped white mark below the eyes. Bright red breast and belly. Narrow pointed black bill. Black legs and feet. Slight crest.

Female: same as male

Juvenile: similar to adult, lacks a red belly

Nest: cup; female builds; 1-2 broods per year

Eggs: 3-4; creamy white with brown markings

Incubation: 13-14 days; female incubates

Fledging: 11-13 days; female and male feed young

Migration: complete, to Mexico

Food: insects

Compare: Smaller than Black Phoebe (pg. 37), which has a white belly. Look for the red belly and breast of Painted Redstart to help identify.

Stan's Notes: A very active bird of woodlands with water nearby. Constantly flits from branch to branch in search of insects. Leans forward, spreads tail and flares wings, flashing its black and white colors. This behavior presumably helps individuals visually locate each other while feeding. Males arrive at breeding sites about one week before the females. Male performs an erratic courtship flight, then chases female. Female builds a cup nest under an overhanging riverbank or cliff. Female broods the young, but both parents feed them. Young of the first clutch disperse quickly while adults start a second clutch. A summer resident, but some stay in western New Mexico during winter.

WHITE-THROATED SWIFT
Aeronautes saxatalis

YEAR-ROUND
SUMMER

Size: 6½" (16 cm)

Male: Black with a white chin, chest and sides of rump. White trailing edge on the length of the first half of wings. Long narrow wings and long thin tail, as seen in flight.

Female: same as male

Juvenile: similar to adult

Nest: cup, in a cavity or crevice; female builds; 1 brood per year

Eggs: 4-5; white without markings

Incubation: unknown days; female incubates

Fledging: unknown days; female and male feed young

Migration: complete, to southern New Mexico, Mexico and Central America

Food: insects

Compare: Similar (but not related) to the Violet-green Swallow (pg. 281), which is smaller and has a green cap and back.

Stan's Notes: A common bird of rocky canyons in elevations from 5,500-8,200 feet (1,700-2,500 m). A perpetual flier, it feeds, bathes and even mates during flight. Pairs press together and spin down through the air, then break apart. Flies in groups, giving twittering calls. Returns in April. Doesn't nest until summertime, when more insects are available to feed to young. Carries food to the young in an expandable throat pouch. Nests in small colonies, constructing cup-shaped nests in rock crevices. Like other swifts, uses its saliva to glue feathers and vegetation into a cup that it seals to the rock.

BLACK PHOEBE
Sayornis nigricans

YEAR-ROUND

Size: 7" (18 cm)

Male: A black head, neck, breast and back with a white belly and undertail. Long narrow tail. Crest makes the head appear pointed. Dark eyes, bill and legs.

Female: same as male

Juvenile: similar to adult, brown-to-tan wing bars

Nest: cup; female builds; 1-2 broods per year

Eggs: 3-6; white without markings

Incubation: 15-17 days; female incubates

Fledging: 14-21 days; female and male feed young

Migration: partial to non-migrator; moves around after breeding to find food

Food: insects

Compare: Distinctive black and white pattern makes identification easy. Watch for tail to pump up and down very quickly when perched. The male Vermilion Flycatcher (pg. 301) is crimson and black. Say's Phoebe (pg. 223) has a pale orange belly and gray head.

Stan's Notes: Often seen in shrubby areas near water. Feeds mostly on insects near the surface of water. In the winter it feeds on insects near the ground. Like other flycatchers, perches on thin branches, flies out to snatch a passing insect and returns to perch. Pumps or bobs tail up and down quickly while perching. Male performs an aerial song and flight with a slow descent to attract a mate. Female builds shallow nest of mud, adhered to rocks or bridges, lined with hair and grass. Often uses same nest or location for several years.

male

female

LADDER-BACKED WOODPECKER
Picoides scalaris

YEAR-ROUND

Size: 7" (18 cm)

Male: Horizontal black-and-white zebra stripes on back, wings and tail. Red crown. Tan breast and belly with black spots. Black eye stripe. Black mustache mark. Dark bill.

Female: same as male, but lacks a red crown

Juvenile: similar to female

Nest: cavity; female and male excavate, then use wood chips to line hole; 1 brood per year

Eggs: 2-4; white without markings

Incubation: 13-15 days; female and male incubate

Fledging: 14-16 days; female and male feed young

Migration: non-migrator

Food: insects, fruit

Compare: Downy Woodpecker (pg. 31) and Hairy Woodpecker (pg. 43) lack zebra striping on their backs.

Stan's Notes: Less common than other woodpeckers of arid desert scrub. Often probes for insects and larvae or feeds on cactus fruit. Male often feeds closer to ground than female; jumps to ground to grab an insect or pecks at the base of shrubs and trees. Female feeds higher up and probes less; pulls bugs from leaves or cracks in bark. A sharp "peek" call and short spurt of drumming. Will drum on a resonant log or tree to advertise territory ownership. Nests in dead branches of mesquite or saguaro cactus. Sometimes will excavate a cavity in a wooden post, yucca plant or utility pole. Common name comes from the black and white striping, resembling ladder rungs.

male

female

RED-NAPED SAPSUCKER
Sphyrapicus nuchalis

Size: 8½" (22 cm)

Male: Black-and-white pattern on back in 2 rows. Red forehead, chin and nape of neck.

Female: same as male, but has white chin and more white on back

Juvenile: brown version of adults, lacking any of the red markings

Nest: cavity; male and female excavate; 1 brood per year

Eggs: 3-7; pale white without markings

Incubation: 12-13 days; female and male incubate

Fledging: 25-29 days; female and male feed young

Migration: complete, to southern New Mexico, Mexico and Central America

Food: insects, tree sap

Compare: The Lewis's Woodpecker (pg. 285) lacks the Red-naped's black-and-white pattern.

Stan's Notes: Closely related to the Yellow-bellied Sapsucker of the eastern U.S. Often associated with aspen, willow and cottonwood trees, nearly always nesting in aspen trees where they are present. Creates several horizontal rows of holes in a tree from which sap oozes. A wide variety of birds and animals use the sap wells that sapsuckers drill. Sapsuckers lap the sap and eat the insects that are also attracted to sap. Cannot suck sap as the name implies; rather, they lap it with their tongues. Some females lack the white chin that helps to differentiate the sexes.

male

female

HAIRY WOODPECKER
Picoides villosus

YEAR-ROUND
MIGRATION

Size: 9" (22.5 cm)

Male: Black-and-white woodpecker with a white belly, and black wings with rows of white spots. White stripe down back. Long black bill. Red mark on back of head.

Female: same as male, but lacks a red mark on head

Juvenile: grayer version of female

Nest: cavity; female and male excavate; 1 brood per year

Eggs: 3-6; white without markings

Incubation: 11-15 days; female and male incubate, the female incubates during day, male at night

Fledging: 28-30 days; male and female feed young

Migration: non-migrator

Food: insects, nuts, seeds; comes to seed and suet feeders

Compare: Larger than Downy Woodpecker (pg. 31) and has a longer bill. The Ladder-backed Woodpecker (pg. 39) has zebra-like stripes.

Stan's Notes: A common woodpecker of wooded backyards that announces its arrival with a sharp chirp before landing on feeders. This bird is responsible for eating many destructive forest insects. Has a barbed tongue, which helps it extract insects from trees. Tiny bristle-like feathers at the base of bill protect the nostrils from wood dust. Drums on hollow logs, branches or stovepipes in springtime to announce its territory. Often prefers to excavate nest cavities in live aspen trees. Has a larger, more oval-shaped cavity entrance than that of Downy Woodpecker.

43

SUMMER

BLACK-NECKED STILT
Himantopus mexicanus

Size: 14" (36 cm)

Male: Upper parts of the head, neck and back are black. Lower parts are white. Ridiculously long red-to-pink legs. Long black bill.

Female: similar to male, only browner on back

Juvenile: similar to female, brown instead of black

Nest: ground; female and male construct; 1 brood per year

Eggs: 3-5; off-white with dark markings

Incubation: 22-26 days; female and male incubate, male incubates during the day, female at night

Fledging: 28-32 days; female and male feed young

Migration: complete, to South America

Food: aquatic insects

Compare: Outrageous length of the red-to-pink legs make this shorebird hard to confuse with any other.

Stan's Notes: A summer resident in parts of New Mexico. It is also found along the West coast and as far north as the Great Lakes. A very vocal bird of shallow marshes, giving a "kek-kek-kek" call. Legs are up to 10 inches (25 cm) long and may be the longest legs in the bird world in proportion to the body. Nests solitarily or in small colonies in open areas. Known for transporting water with water-soaked belly feathers (belly-soaking) to cool eggs during hot weather. Aggressively defends its nest, eggs and young. The young leave the nest shortly after hatching.

female pg. 163

male

LESSER SCAUP
Aythya affinis

MIGRATION
WINTER

Size: 16-17" (40-43 cm)

Male: Appears mostly black with bold white sides and gray back. Chest and head look nearly black, but head appears purple with green highlights in direct sun. Bright yellow eyes.

Female: overall brown with dull white patch at base of light gray bill, yellow eyes

Juvenile: same as female

Nest: ground; female builds; 1 brood per year

Eggs: 8-14; olive buff without markings

Incubation: 22-28 days; female incubates

Fledging: 45-50 days; female teaches young to feed

Migration: complete, to southwestern states, Mexico, Central America, northern South America

Food: aquatic plants and insects

Compare: The male Ring-necked Duck (pg. 49) has a bold white ring around its bill, a black back and lacks the bold white sides of the male Lesser Scaup. The male Blue-winged Teal (pg. 161) is smaller and has a bright white crescent-shaped patch near the base of bill.

Stan's Notes: Common diving duck. Often in large flocks on lakes, ponds and sewage lagoons. Submerges to feed on bottom of lakes (unlike dabbling ducks, which tip forward to reach bottom). Note the bold white stripe under wings when in flight. Male leaves female when she starts to incubate her eggs. Quantity of eggs (clutch size) increases with age of female. Interesting baby-sitting arrangement in which groups of young (crèches) are tended by 1-3 adult females.

female pg. 165

male

RING-NECKED DUCK
Aythya collaris

Size: 17" (43 cm)

Male: A striking duck with black head, chest and back. Sides are gray to nearly white. A light blue bill with a bold white ring and second ring at base of bill. Top of head is peaked.

Female: dark brown back, light brown sides, a gray face, dark brown crown, white line behind eyes, white ring around a light blue bill, top of head is peaked

Juvenile: similar to female

Nest: ground; female builds; 1 brood per year

Eggs: 8-10; olive gray to brown without markings

Incubation: 26-27 days; female incubates

Fledging: 49-56 days; female teaches young to feed

Migration: complete migrator, to southwestern states, Mexico and Central America

Food: aquatic plants and insects

Compare: Similar size as male Lesser Scaup (pg. 47), which has a gray back unlike the black back of male Ring-necked Duck. Look for male Ring-necked's bold white ring around bill.

Stan's Notes: A common winter duck in New Mexico. Usually is seen in larger freshwater lakes. A diving duck, watch for it to dive underwater to forage for food. Takes to flight by springing up off water. Was named "Ring-necked" because of the cinnamon collar (nearly impossible to see in the field). Also called Ring-billed Duck due to the white ring on its bill, and Blue Bill by duck hunters.

winter

breeding

AMERICAN AVOCET
Recurvirostra americana

MIGRATION
SUMMER

Size: 18" (45 cm)

Male: Black and white back, white belly. A long, thin upturned bill and long gray legs. Head and neck rusty red during breeding, gray in the winter.

Female: similar to male, only with a more strongly upturned bill

Juvenile: similar to adults, with a slight wash of rusty red on neck and head

Nest: ground; female and male construct; 1 brood per year

Eggs: 3-5; light olive with brown markings

Incubation: 22-29 days; female and male incubate

Fledging: 28-35 days; female and male feed young

Migration: complete, to Mexico

Food: insects, crustaceans, aquatic vegetation and fruit

Compare: One of the few long-legged shorebirds in New Mexico. Look for the rusty red head of the breeding Avocet and long upturned bill.

Stan's Notes: A handsome long-legged bird that prefers shallow alkaline, saline or brackish water, it is well adapted to arid western U.S. conditions. Uses its up-curved bill to sweep from side to side across mud bottoms in search of insects. Both the male and female have a brood patch to incubate eggs and brood their young. Nests in loose colonies of up to 20 pairs. All members of the colony will defend together against intruders.

male

female pg. 169

COMMON GOLDENEYE
Bucephala clangula

WINTER

Size: 18½-20" (47-50 cm)

Male: A mostly white duck with a black back and large, puffy green head. Large white spot in front of each bright golden eye. Dark bill.

Female: brown and gray, a large dark brown head, gray body, white collar, bright golden eyes, yellow-tipped dark bill

Juvenile: same as female, but has a dark bill

Nest: cavity; female lines old woodpecker cavity; 1 brood per year

Eggs: 8-10; light green without markings

Incubation: 28-32 days; female incubates

Fledging: 56-59 days; female leads young to food

Migration: complete, to southwestern states, Mexico

Food: aquatic plants, insects

Compare: Similar to, but larger than, the black and white male Lesser Scaup (pg. 47). Look for the distinctive white mark in front of each golden eye, and a white chest.

Stan's Notes: Known for its loud whistling, produced by its wings in flight. In late winter and early spring, male often attracts female through elaborate displays, throwing its head backward while it utters a single raspy note. Female will lay eggs in other goldeneye nests, which results in some mothers incubating up to 30 eggs. Received the common name from its obvious bright golden eyes. Winters in New Mexico where it finds open water.

BLACK-BILLED MAGPIE
Pica hudsonia

Size: 20" (50 cm)

Male: A large black-and-white bird with very long tail and white belly. Iridescent green wings and tail in direct sunlight. Large black bill and legs. White wing patches flash in flight.

Female: same as male

Juvenile: same as adult, but shorter tail

Nest: modified pendulous; the female and male build; 1 brood per year

Eggs: 5-8; green with brown markings

Incubation: 16-21 days; female incubates

Fledging: 25-29 days; female and male feed young

Migration: non-migrator

Food: insects, carrion, fruit, seeds

Compare: Larger than the Common Grackle (pg. 17). Contrasting black-and-white colors and the very long tail of Magpie distinguish it from the all-black American Crow (pg. 23).

Stan's Notes: A wonderfully intelligent bird that is able to mimic dogs, cats and even people. Will often raid a barnyard dog dish for food. Feeds on a variety of food from road kill to insects and seeds it collects from the ground. Easily identified by its bold black-and-white colors and long streaming tail. Travels in small flocks, usually family members, and tends to be very gregarious. Breeds in small colonies. Unusual dome nest (dome-shaped roof) deep within thick shrubs. Mates with same mate for several years. Prefers open fields with cattle or sheep, where it feeds on insects attracted to livestock.

BLACK-CROWNED NIGHT-HERON
Nycticorax nycticorax

YEAR-ROUND
MIGRATION
SUMMER

Size: 22-27" (56-69 cm); up to 3½-foot wingspan

Male: A stocky, hunched and inactive heron with black back and crown, white belly and gray wings. Long dark bill, short yellow legs and bright red eyes. Breeding adult has 2 long white plumes on crown.

Female: same as male

Juvenile: golden brown head and back with white spots, streaked breast, yellow orange eyes, brown bill

Nest: platform; female and male build; 1 brood per year

Eggs: 3-5; light blue without markings

Incubation: 24-26 days; female and male incubate

Fledging: 42-48 days; female and male feed young

Migration: complete migrator, to southwestern states, Mexico and Central America, non-migrator in parts of New Mexico

Food: fish, aquatic insects

Compare: Half the size of Great Blue Heron (pg. 275) when perching. Look for a short-necked heron with a black back and crown.

Stan's Notes: A very secretive bird, this heron is most active near dawn and dusk (crepuscular). It hunts alone, but nests in small colonies. Roosts in trees during the day. Often squawks if disturbed from the daytime roost. Often seen being harassed by other herons during days.

soaring

juvenile

soaring juvenile

BALD EAGLE
Haliaeetus leucocephalus

YEAR-ROUND
WINTER

Size: 31-37" (79-94 cm); up to 7-foot wingspan

Male: Pure white head and tail contrast with dark brown-to-black body and wings. A large, curved yellow bill and yellow feet.

Female: same as male, only slightly larger

Juvenile: dark brown with white spots or speckles throughout body and wings, gray bill

Nest: massive platform, usually in a tree; female and male build; 1 brood per year

Eggs: 2; off-white without markings

Incubation: 34-36 days; female and male incubate

Fledging: 75-90 days; female and male feed young

Migration: partial to complete, to southwestern states

Food: fish, carrion, birds (mainly ducks)

Compare: Golden Eagle (pg. 197) and Turkey Vulture (pg. 29) lack the white head and white tail of adult Bald Eagle. Juvenile Golden Eagle, with its white wrist marks and white base of tail, is similar to the juvenile Bald Eagle.

Stan's Notes: Driven to near extinction due to DDT poisoning and illegal killing. Now making a comeback in North America. Returns to same nest each year, adding more sticks, enlarging it to massive proportions, at times up to 1,000 pounds (450 kg). In the midair mating ritual, one eagle will flip upside down and lock talons with another. Both tumble, then break apart to continue flight. Thought to mate for life, but will switch mates if not successful reproducing. Juvenile attains the white head and tail at about 4-5 years of age. A winter resident in most of New Mexico.

59

BLUE-GRAY GNATCATCHER
Polioptila caerulea

YEAR-ROUND
MIGRATION
SUMMER

Size: 4" (10 cm)

Male: A light blue-to-gray head, back, breast and wings, with a black forehead and eyebrows. White belly and prominent white eye-ring. Long black tail with a white undertail, often held cocked above the rest of body.

Female: same as male, only grayer and lacking black on head

Juvenile: similar to female

Nest: cup; female and male build; 1 brood a year

Eggs: 4-5; pale blue with dark markings

Incubation: 10-13 days; female and male incubate

Fledging: 10-12 days; female and male feed young

Migration: complete, to Mexico and Central America

Food: insects

Compare: The only small blue bird with a black tail. Constantly flicks its tail up and down and from side to side. Very active near the nest, look for it flitting around upper branches in search of insects.

Stan's Notes: Found in a wide variety of forest types throughout New Mexico. It has increased and expanded its range northward along the eastern slope of the Rocky Mountains over the past few decades. Listen for its wheezy call notes to help locate. A fun and easy bird to watch as it cocks and fans tail while calling. Like many other open woodland nesting birds, it is a common cowbird host. Returns to the state by mid-April, with most leaving by late August. A few winter in southern New Mexico.

female pg. 97

male

INDIGO BUNTING
Passerina cyanea

MIGRATION
SUMMER

Size: 5½" (14 cm)

Male: Vibrant blue finch-like bird. Scattered dark markings on wings and tail.

Female: light brown bird with faint markings

Juvenile: similar to female

Nest: cup; female builds; 2 broods per year

Eggs: 3-4; pale blue without markings

Incubation: 12-13 days; female incubates

Fledging: 10-11 days; female feeds young

Migration: complete, to Mexico, Central America and South America

Food: insects, seeds, fruit; will visit seed feeders

Compare: Male Mountain Bluebird (pg. 75) is larger and has a thin black bill and white lower belly. Male Western Bluebird (pg. 73) is also larger and has a rusty red breast.

Stan's Notes: Usually only the males are noticed. Actually a black bird, as it doesn't have any blue pigment in its feathers. As with the Blue Jay, sunlight is refracted within the structure of the bunting's feathers, making them appear blue. Appears iridescent in direct sun. Molts to acquire body feathers with gray tips, which quickly wear off to reveal bright blue plumage in spring. Molts in fall to appear like females during winter. Males often sing from treetops to attract mates. Will come to feeders in spring before insects are plentiful. Mostly seen along woodland edges, feeding on insects. Migrates at night in flocks of 5-10 individuals. A late migrant, males return before females and juveniles, usually returning to previous year's nest site. Juveniles move to within a mile from birth site.

female pg. 99

male

LAZULI BUNTING
Passerina amoena

MIGRATION
SUMMER

Size: 5½" (14 cm)

Male: A turquoise blue head, neck, back and tail. Cinnamon chest with cinnamon extending down flanks slightly. White belly. Two bold white wing bars. Non-breeding male has a spotty blue head and back.

Female: overall grayish brown, warm brown breast, a light wash of blue on wings and tail, gray throat, light gray belly and 2 narrow white wing bars

Juvenile: similar to adult of the same sex

Nest: cup; female builds; 2-3 broods per year

Eggs: 3-5; pale blue without markings

Incubation: 11-13 days; female incubates

Fledging: 10-12 days; female and male feed young

Migration: complete, to Mexico

Food: insects, seeds

Compare: The male Indigo Bunting (pg. 63) lacks the male Lazuli's multicolored plumage. Male Western Bluebird (pg. 73) is darker blue. Male Blue Grosbeak (pg. 71) has chestnut wing bars and lacks a white belly.

Stan's Notes: More common in shrub lands in New Mexico. Does not like dense forests. Has a strong association with water such as rivers and streams. Gathers in small flocks and tends to move up in elevations after breeding to hunt for insects and search for seeds. It has increased in population and expanded its range over the last 100 years.

TREE SWALLOW
Tachycineta bicolor

Size: 5-6" (13-15 cm)

Male: Blue green in the spring and greener in fall. Appears to change color in direct sunlight. A white belly, a notched tail and pointed wing tips.

Female: similar to male, only duller

Juvenile: gray brown with a white belly and grayish breast band

Nest: cavity; female and male line former woodpecker cavity or nest box; 1 brood per year

Eggs: 4-6; white without markings

Incubation: 13-16 days; female incubates

Fledging: 20-24 days; female and male feed young

Migration: complete, to Mexico and Central America

Food: insects

Compare: Barn Swallow (pg. 69) has a rust belly and deeply forked tail. Similar size as the Cliff Swallow (pg. 101) and Violet-green Swallow (pg. 281), but lacks any tan-to-rust color of the Cliff Swallow and any emerald green of the Violet-green Swallow.

Stan's Notes: The first swallow species to return each spring. Most common along ponds, lakes and agricultural fields. Is attracted to your yard with a nest box. Competes with Western and Mountain Bluebirds for cavities and nest boxes. Travels great distances to find dropped feathers to line its grass nest. Sometimes seen playing, chasing after dropped feathers. Often seen flying back and forth across fields, feeding on insects. Gathers in large flocks to migrate.

BARN SWALLOW
Hirundo rustica

Size: 7" (18 cm)

Male: A sleek swallow with a blue black back, a cinnamon belly and a reddish brown chin. White spots on long forked tail.

Female: same as male, only slightly duller

Juvenile: similar to adults, with a tan belly and chin, and shorter tail

Nest: cup; female and male construct; 2 broods per year

Eggs: 4-5; white with brown markings

Incubation: 13-17 days; female incubates

Fledging: 18-23 days; female and male feed young

Migration: complete, to South America

Food: insects, prefers beetles, wasps and flies

Compare: Tree Swallow (pg. 67) has a white belly and chin and a notched tail. Larger than the Cliff Swallow (pg. 99) and Violet-green Swallow (pg. 281), which both lack the distinctive, deeply forked tail. Violet-green Swallow is distinctively green with a white face.

Stan's Notes: Of the seven swallow species in New Mexico, this is the only one with a deeply forked tail. Unlike other swallows, Barn Swallows rarely glide in flight, so look for continuous flapping. It builds a mud nest using up to 1,000 beak-loads of mud, often in or on barns. Nests in colonies of 4-6 individuals, but nesting alone isn't uncommon. Drinks in flight, skimming water or getting water from wet leaves. Also bathes while flying through rain or sprinklers.

female
pg. 121

male

SUMMER

BLUE GROSBEAK
Passerina caerulea

Size: 7" (18 cm)

Male: Overall blue bird with 2 chestnut wing bars. Large gray-to-silver bill. Black around base of bill.

Female: overall brown with darker wings and tail, 2 tan wing bars, large gray-to-silver bill

Juvenile: similar to female

Nest: cup; female builds; 1-2 broods per year

Eggs: 3-6; pale blue without markings

Incubation: 11-12 days; female incubates

Fledging: 9-10 days; female and male feed young

Migration: complete, to Mexico and Central America

Food: insects, seeds; will come to seed feeders

Compare: The male Lazuli Bunting (pg. 65) has 2 bold white wing bars and a white belly. The male Indigo Bunting (pg. 63) is smaller and lacks wing bars. The male Western and Mountain Bluebirds (pp. 73 and 75, respectively) are the same size, but lack the male Grosbeak's chestnut wing bars and oversized bill.

Stan's Notes: This bird returns to New Mexico by early May. It has expanded northward with overall populations increasing over the past 30-40 years. A bird of semi-open habitats such as overgrown fields, riversides, woodland edges and fencerows. Frequently seen twitching and spreading its tail. First-year males show only some blue, obtaining the full complement of blue feathers in the second winter. Visits seed feeders.

male

female

WESTERN BLUEBIRD
Sialia mexicana

YEAR-ROUND
WINTER

Size: 7" (18 cm)

Male: Deep blue head, neck, throat, back, wings and tail. Rusty red chest and flanks.

Female: similar to male, only duller with gray head

Juvenile: similar to female, with a speckled chest

Nest: cavity, old woodpecker cavity, wooden nest box; female builds; 1-2 broods per year

Eggs: 4-6; pale blue without markings

Incubation: 13-14 days; female incubates

Fledging: 22-23 days; female and male feed young

Migration: complete, to southwestern states, Mexico

Food: insects, fruit

Compare: Mountain Bluebird (pg. 75) is similar, but lacks the rusty red breast. Larger than male Lazuli Bunting (pg. 65), which has white wing bars. Same size as male Blue Grosbeak (pg. 71), but lacks the Grosbeak's chestnut wing bars and oversized bill.

Stan's Notes: Not as common as the Mountain Bluebird. Found in a variety of habitats, from agricultural land to clear-cuts. Requires a cavity for nesting. Competes with starlings for nest cavities. Like the Mountain Bluebird, it uses nest boxes, which are responsible for the stable populations. Courting male will fly in front of female, spreading wings and tail, then perch next to her. Often seen going in and out of nest box or cavity as if to say, "Look inside." Male may offer food to female to establish pair bond.

male

female

MOUNTAIN BLUEBIRD
Sialia currucoides

Size: 7" (18 cm)

Male: An overall sky blue bird with a darker blue head, back, wings and tail and white lower belly. Thin black bill.

Female: similar to male, but paler with a nearly gray head and chest and a whitish belly

Juvenile: similar to adult of the same sex

Nest: cavity, old woodpecker cavity, wooden nest box; female builds; 1-2 broods per year

Eggs: 4-6; pale blue without markings

Incubation: 13-14 days; female incubates

Fledging: 22-23 days; female and male feed young

Migration: complete, to southwestern states, Mexico

Food: insects

Compare: Similar to Western Bluebird (pg. 73), but not as dark blue and lacks Western's rusty red chest. Male Indigo Bunting (pg. 63) is smaller and lacks a white lower belly. Male Blue Grosbeak (pg. 71) has chestnut wing bars and an oversized bill.

Stan's Notes: This bird is common in open mountainous country. Due to conservation of suitable nest sites (dead trees with cavities and man-made nesting boxes), populations increased dramatically over the past 30 years. Like other bluebirds, Mountain Bluebirds take well to nesting boxes and tolerate close contact with humans. Young imprint on their first nesting box or cavity, then choose a similar type of box or cavity throughout the rest of life.

WESTERN SCRUB-JAY
Aphelocoma californica

YEAR-ROUND

Size: 11" (28 cm)

Male: Blue head, wings, tail and breast band with a brownish patch on back. Dull white chin, breast and belly. Very long tail.

Female: same as male

Juvenile: similar to adult, overall gray with light blue wings and tail

Nest: cup; female and male construct; 1 brood per year

Eggs: 3-6; pale green with red brown markings

Incubation: 15-17 days; female incubates

Fledging: 18-20 days; female and male feed young

Migration: non-migrator

Food: insects, seeds, fruit; comes to seed feeders

Compare: Same size as the Pinyon Jay (pg. 79), which lacks the white chest and belly. Same size as the Steller's Jay (pg. 81), but lacks the black head and pointed crest. Gray Jay (pg. 255) is gray and white, lacking any of Western Scrub-Jay's blue color.

Stan's Notes: A tame bird of urban areas that visits feeders. Several subspecies occur with some regional variations in color, the Interior race (shown) being a paler blue. Forms a long-term pair bond, with the male feeding female before and during incubation. Young of a pair remain close by for up to a couple years, helping parents raise subsequent brothers and sisters. Caches food by burying it for later consumption. Likely serves as a major distributor of oaks and pines by not returning to eat the seeds it buried.

PINYON JAY
Gymnorhinus cyanocephalus

Size: 11" (28 cm)

Male: A short-tailed dull blue jay. Head is darker blue than rest of body. Faint white streaks on chin. Long, pointed black bill. Black legs.

Female: same as male

Juvenile: overall gray with blue highlights

Nest: cup; female and male construct; 1-2 broods per year

Eggs: 4-5; blue, green, gray or white with brown markings

Incubation: 16-17 days; female incubates

Fledging: 19-21 days; female and male feed young

Migration: non-migrator

Food: seeds, insects, fruit

Compare: The Western Scrub-Jay (pg. 77) has a white chest and belly. Steller's Jay (pg. 81) has a black head and crest. Gray Jay (pg. 255) is gray with a mostly white head.

Stan's Notes: Highly specialized jay, usually seen near piñon pine trees. Gathers nuts from piñon cones, storing them in large caches often on the ground. An important seed disperser, with forgotten caches sprouting into new trees. Can breed in late winter in years with abundant seed production. Gregarious, it breeds in colonies of up to 50 pairs. Starts breeding at age 3. Mates often the same age stay together for years. In winter flocks of up to several hundred gather to roost and find food, and move on when supplies are low. A soft flight song, "hoyi-hoyi-hoyi-hoyi." Often walks rather than hops, like most other jays. Closely related to Clark's Nutcracker.

STELLER'S JAY
Cyanocitta stelleri

Size: 11" (28 cm)

Male: Dark blue wings, tail and belly. Black head, nape of the neck and chest. Large, pointed black crest on head that can be lifted at will. Distinctive white streaks on forehead and just above eyes.

Female: same as male

Juvenile: similar to adult, lacking white markings on the forehead and white eye stripe

Nest: cup; female and male build; 1 brood a year

Eggs: 3-5; pale green with brown markings

Incubation: 14-16 days; female incubates

Fledging: 16-18 days; female and male feed young

Migration: non-migrator

Food: insects, berries, seeds; will visit seed feeders

Compare: The Western Scrub-Jay (pg. 77) and Pinyon Jay (pg. 79) are the same size, but lack the black head and crest of the Steller's Jay. Gray Jay (pg. 255) lacks any blue and a crest.

Stan's Notes: Common resident of foothills and lower mountains from 6,000-8,000 feet (1,850-2,450 m). Usually seen in coniferous forests. Rarely competes with the Gray Jay, which occupies higher elevations. Thought to mate for life. Rarely disperses very far, often breeding within 10 miles (16 km) of birthplace. Several subspecies found throughout the Rocky Mountains. The New Mexico form has a black crest with distinctive white streaks. Other varieties lack the white markings. Named after Arctic explorer Georg W. Steller, who is said to have discovered the bird on the coast of Alaska in 1741.

male

female

BELTED KINGFISHER
Ceryle alcyon

YEAR-ROUND
WINTER

Size: 13" (33 cm)

Male: Large blue bird with white belly. Broad blue gray breast band and a ragged crest that is raised and lowered at will. Large head with a long, thick black bill. A small white spot directly in front of red brown eyes. Black wing tips with splashes of white that flash when flying.

Female: same as male, but with rusty breast band in addition to blue gray band, and rusty flanks

Juvenile: similar to female

Nest: cavity; female and male excavate; 1 brood per year

Eggs: 6-7; white without markings

Incubation: 23-24 days; female and male incubate

Fledging: 23-24 days; female and male feed young

Migration: complete migrator, to southwestern states, Mexico, Central and South America

Food: small fish

Compare: Larger than the Western Scrub-Jay (pg. 77). Kingfisher is rarely found away from water.

Stan's Notes: Seen perched on branches near the water, it dives headfirst for small fish and returns to a branch to eat. Has a loud machine-gun-like call. Excavates a deep cavity in bank of river or lake. Parents drop dead fish into water, teaching the young to dive. Regurgitates pellets of bone after meals, being unable to pass bones through digestive tract. Mates recognize each other by call. Many northern birds move into the state in winter, increasing populations.

HOUSE WREN
Troglodytes aedon

YEAR-ROUND
MIGRATION
SUMMER
WINTER

Size: 5" (13 cm)

Male: A small all-brown bird with lighter brown markings on tail and wings. Slightly curved brown bill. Often holds its tail erect.

Female: same as male

Juvenile: same as adult

Nest: cavity; female and male line just about any nest cavity; 2 broods per year

Eggs: 4-6; tan with brown markings

Incubation: 10-13 days; female and male incubate

Fledging: 12-15 days; female and male feed young

Migration: complete, to southern New Mexico, Mexico

Food: insects

Compare: Smaller than Bewick's Wren, Canyon Wren, and Rock Wren (pp. 103, 105 and 107, respectively). Bewick's Wren has white eyebrows. Canyon Wren has a white throat and breast. Rock Wren has fine white speckles on the back and a light tan belly and breast.

Stan's Notes: A prolific songster, it will sing from dawn until dusk during the mating season. Easily attracted to nest boxes. In spring, the male chooses several prospective nesting cavities and places a few small twigs in each. Female inspects each, chooses one, and finishes the nest building. She will completely fill the nest cavity with uniformly small twigs, then line a small depression at back of cavity with pine needles and grass. Often has trouble fitting long twigs through nest cavity hole. Tries many different directions and approaches until successful.

PINE SISKIN
Carduelis pinus

YEAR-ROUND
WINTER

Size: 5" (13 cm)

Male: Small brown finch. Heavily streaked back, breast and belly. Yellow wing bars. Yellow at base of tail. Thin bill.

Female: same as male

Juvenile: similar to adult, light yellow tinge over the breast and chin

Nest: modified cup; female constructs; 2 broods per year

Eggs: 3-4; greenish blue with brown markings

Incubation: 12-13 days; female incubates

Fledging: 14-15 days; female and male feed young

Migration: irruptive; moves around the state in search of food

Food: seeds, insects; will come to seed feeders

Compare: Female American Goldfinch (pg. 319) and Lesser Goldfinch (pg. 317) lack streaks and have white wing bars. Female House Finch (pg. 89) has a streaked chest, but lacks Pine Siskin's yellow wing bars.

Stan's Notes: A nesting resident, it is usually considered a winter finch because it is more visible in the non-nesting season, when it gathers in flocks, moves around the state and visits feeders. Comes to thistle feeders. Travels and breeds in small groups. Male feeds the female during incubation. Juveniles lose yellow tint by late summer of the first year. Builds its nest toward ends of coniferous branches, where needles are dense, helping to conceal. Nests are often only a few feet apart.

male
pg. 299

female

HOUSE FINCH
Carpodacus mexicanus

Size: 5" (13 cm)

Female: A plain brown bird with a heavily streaked white chest.

Male: orange red face, chest and rump, a brown cap, brown marking behind eyes, brown wings streaked with white, streaked belly

Juvenile: similar to female

Nest: cup, sometimes in cavities; female builds; 2 broods per year

Eggs: 4-5; pale blue, lightly marked

Incubation: 12-14 days; female incubates

Fledging: 15-19 days; female and male feed young

Migration: non-migrator to partial migrator; will move around to find food

Food: seeds, fruit, leaf buds; will visit seed feeders

Compare: Female Cassin's Finch (pg. 111) has a more heavily streaked belly. Similar to Pine Siskin (pg. 87), but lacks yellow wing bars and has a larger bill. Female Goldfinches (pp. 317 and 319) have unmarked breasts.

Stan's Notes: Very social bird. Visits feeders in small flocks. Likes nesting in hanging flower baskets. Incubating female is fed by the male. Has a loud, cheerful warbling song. Historically it occurred from the Pacific coast to the Rockies, with only a few reaching the eastern side. House Finches that were originally introduced to Long Island, New York, from the western U.S. in the 1940s have since populated the entire eastern U.S. Now found all over the country. Suffers from a fatal eye disease that causes eyes to crust over.

CHIPPING SPARROW
Spizella passerina

Size: 5" (13 cm)

Male: Small gray brown sparrow with a clear gray breast, rusty crown and white eyebrows. A black eye line and thin gray black bill. Two faint wing bars.

Female: same as male

Juvenile: similar to adult, has a streaked breast, lacks the rusty crown

Nest: cup; female builds; 2 broods per year

Eggs: 3-5; blue green with brown markings

Incubation: 11-14 days; female incubates

Fledging: 10-12 days; female and male feed young

Migration: complete, to southern New Mexico, Mexico and Central America

Food: insects, seeds; will come to ground feeders

Compare: Lark Sparrow (pg. 113) is larger and has a white chest and central spot. Song Sparrow (pg. 93) has a heavily streaked breast. Fox Sparrow (pg. 119) is larger and lacks the rusty crown. Female House Finch (pg. 89) has a streaked chest.

Stan's Notes: A common garden or yard bird, often seen feeding on dropped seeds beneath feeders. Gathers in large family groups to feed in preparation for migration. Migrates at night in flocks of 20-30 birds. The common name comes from the male's slow "chip" call. Often is just called Chippy. Nest is placed low in dense shrubs and is almost always lined with animal hair. Can be very unafraid of people, allowing you to approach closely before it flies away.

YEAR-ROUND
WINTER

SONG SPARROW
Melospiza melodia

Size: 5-6" (13-15 cm)

Male: Common brown sparrow with heavy dark streaks on breast coalescing into a central dark spot.

Female: same as male

Juvenile: similar to adult, finely streaked breast, lacks a central spot

Nest: cup; female builds; 2 broods per year

Eggs: 3-4; pale blue to green with reddish brown markings

Incubation: 12-14 days; female incubates

Fledging: 9-12 days; female and male feed young

Migration: complete to non-migrator in New Mexico

Food: insects, seeds; rarely visits seed feeders

Compare: Similar to other brown sparrows. Look for a heavily streaked chest with central dark spot.

Stan's Notes: Many Song Sparrow subspecies or varieties, but dark central spot carries through each variant. While the female builds another nest for a second brood, the male sparrow often takes over feeding the young. Returns to a similar area each year, defending a small territory by singing from thick shrubs. A common host of the Brown-headed Cowbird. Ground feeders, look for them to scratch simultaneously with both feet to expose seeds. Unlike many other sparrow species, Song Sparrows rarely flock together. A constant songster, repeating its loud, clear song every couple minutes. Song varies in structure, but is basically the same from region to region.

male pg. 211

female

pink-sided

Oregon female

DARK-EYED JUNCO
Junco hyemalis

Size: 5½" (14 cm)

Female: Round, dark-eyed bird with a tan-to-brown chest, head and back. White belly. Ivory-to-pink bill. Since the outermost tail feathers are white, tail appears as a white V in flight.

Male: same as female, only slate gray to charcoal

Juvenile: similar to female, but has a streaked breast and head

Nest: cup; female and male construct; 2 broods per year

Eggs: 3-5; white with reddish brown markings

Incubation: 12-13 days; female incubates

Fledging: 10-13 days; male and female feed young

Migration: partial to non-migrator in New Mexico

Food: seeds, insects; will come to seed feeders

Compare: Rarely confused with any other bird. Small flocks feed under bird feeders in winter.

Stan's Notes: Several junco species have now been combined into one, simply called Dark-eyed Junco (see inset photos). A common year-round resident and one of the most numerous wintering birds in New Mexico. Females tend to migrate farther south than males. Spends the winter in foothills and plains after snowmelt; returns to higher elevations to nest. Nests in a wide variety of wooded habitats in April and May. Adhering to a rigid social hierarchy, dominant birds chase the less dominant birds. Look for its white outer tail feathers flashing in flight. Most comfortable on the ground, juncos "double-scratch" with both feet to expose seeds and insects. Eats many weed seeds. Usually is seen on the ground in small flocks.

female

male pg. 63

MIGRATION
SUMMER

Size: 5½" (14 cm)

Female: Light brown finch-like bird. Faint streaking on a light tan chest. Wings have a very faint blue cast with indistinct wing bars.

Male: vibrant blue finch-like bird, scattered dark markings on wings and tail

Juvenile: similar to female

Nest: cup; female builds; 2 broods per year

Eggs: 3-4; pale blue without markings

Incubation: 12-13 days; female incubates

Fledging: 10-11 days; female feeds young

Migration: complete, to Mexico, Central America and South America

Food: insects, seeds, fruit; will visit seed feeders

Compare: Extremely similar to female Lazuli Bunting (pg. 99), which has more defined wing bars. Female Blue Grosbeak (pg. 121) is larger and has tan wing bars. Female American Goldfinch (pg. 319) has white wing bars. Female House Finch (pg. 89) has a heavily streaked chest.

Stan's Notes: A secretive bird, usually only the male buntings are seen. Males often sing from treetops to attract mates. Will come to feeders in the spring before insects are plentiful. Mostly seen along woodland edges, feeding on insects. Migrates at night in flocks of 5-10 individuals. A late migrant, males return before females and juveniles, usually returning to the previous year's nest site. Juveniles move to within a mile from birth site.

male pg. 65

female

LAZULI BUNTING
Passerina amoena

MIGRATION
SUMMER

Size: 5½" (14 cm)

Female: Overall grayish brown with a warm brown chest, light wash of blue on wings and tail, gray throat and light gray belly. Two narrow white wing bars.

Male: turquoise blue head, neck, back and tail, cinnamon breast, white belly, 2 bold white wing bars

Juvenile: similar to adult of the same sex

Nest: cup; female builds; 2-3 broods per year

Eggs: 3-5; pale blue without markings

Incubation: 11-13 days; female incubates

Fledging: 10-12 days; female and male feed young

Migration: complete, to Mexico

Food: insects, seeds

Compare: Female Indigo Bunting (pg. 97) is the same size, but has faint streaking on the breast and less obvious wing bars. Female Blue Grosbeak (pg. 121) is overall darker and has tan wing bars. Female Western Bluebird (pg. 73) and Mountain Bluebird (pg. 75) are larger and have much more blue.

Stan's Notes: More common in shrub lands in New Mexico. Does not like dense forests. Has a strong association with water such as rivers and streams. Gathers in small flocks and tends to move up in elevations after breeding to hunt for insects and search for seeds. It has increased in population and expanded its range over the last 100 years.

CLIFF SWALLOW
Petrochelidon pyrrhonota

Size: 5½" (14 cm)

Male: A uniquely patterned swallow with a dark back, wings and cap. Distinctive tan-to-rust rump, cheeks and forehead.

Female: same as male

Juvenile: similar to adult, lacks distinct patterning

Nest: gourd-shaped, made of mud; the male and female build; 1-2 broods per year

Eggs: 3-6; pale white with brown markings

Incubation: 14-16 days; male and female incubate

Fledging: 21-24 days; female and male feed young

Migration: complete, to South America

Food: insects

Compare: Smaller than Barn Swallow (pg. 69), which has a deeply forked tail and blue back and wings. The Tree Swallow (pg. 67) lacks any tan-to-rust coloring. Violet-green Swallow (pg. 281) is green with a bright white face.

Stan's Notes: A common and widespread swallow species in New Mexico in summer. Common around bridges (especially bridges over water) and rural housing (especially in open country close to cliffs). Constructs a gourd-shaped nest with a funnel-like entrance pointing down. A colony nester, with many nests lined up beneath eaves of buildings or under cliff overhangs. Will carry balls of mud up to a mile to construct its nest. Many of the colony return to the same nest sites each year. Not unusual for it to have two broods per season. If the number of nests beneath eaves becomes a problem, wait until after young have left the nests to hose off the mud.

BEWICK'S WREN
Thryomanes bewickii

YEAR-ROUND
MIGRATION

Size: 5½" (14 cm)

Male: Brown cap, back, wings and tail. Gray chest and belly. White chin and eyebrows. Long tail with white spots on edges is cocked and flits sideways. Pointed down-curved bill.

Female: same as male

Juvenile: similar to adult

Nest: cavity; female and male build nest in woodpecker hole or nest box; 2-3 broods a year

Eggs: 4-8; white with brown markings

Incubation: 12-14 days; female incubates

Fledging: 10-14 days; female and male feed young

Migration: non-migrator to partial migrator; will move around to find food

Food: insects, seeds

Compare: House Wren (pg. 85) is slightly smaller and lacks the obvious white eyebrow markings and white spots on the tail. The Rock Wren (pg. 107) has a gray back with white spots.

Stan's Notes: A common wren of backyards and gardens. Insects make up 97 percent of its diet, with plant seeds composing the rest. Competes with House Wrens for nesting cavities. Male will choose nesting cavities and start to build nests using small uniform-sized sticks. Female will make the final selection of a nest site and finish building. Begins breeding in April. Has 2-3 broods per year. Male feeds female while she incubates. Average size territory per pair is 5 acres (2 ha), which they defend all year long.

CANYON WREN
Catherpes mexicanus

YEAR-ROUND

Size: 5¾" (14.5 cm)

Male: Chestnut back, wings, belly and tail. Gray head and nape of neck. A distinctive white throat and chest. Long downward-curving bill. Tail often cocked up.

Female: same as male

Juvenile: similar to adult

Nest: crevice; male and female build; 1-2 broods per year

Eggs: 4-6; white with light brown markings

Incubation: 14-16 days; female and male incubate

Fledging: 14-18 days; female and male feed young

Migration: non-migrator to partial migrator; will move around to find food

Food: insects

Compare: Slightly smaller than Rock Wren (pg. 107), which tends to be more grayish and has a duller white chin. Slightly larger than the House Wren (pg. 85), which lacks the large bill of the Canyon Wren.

Stan's Notes: An active wren, spending its entire life among rocks and cliffs. Prefers steep-sided canyons, hence its common name. Maintains winter territories usually around running water to hunt for winter-active insects. Territories are up to 2 acres (1 ha) in size. Nests are attached to rocks within crevices that usually have some kind of rock covering. May reuse the nest from year to year. Lives in close association with Rock Wrens, which use scattered boulders and rocks for nesting.

ROCK WREN
Salpinctes obsoletus

YEAR-ROUND
MIGRATION

Size: 6" (15 cm)

Male: Overall grayish brown with tinges of buffy brown on tail and wings. Gray back, often finely speckled with white. Belly and breast are light tan.

Female: same as male

Juvenile: similar to adult

Nest: crevice; male and female build; 1-2 broods per year

Eggs: 4-8; white with light brown markings

Incubation: 14-16 days; female and male incubate

Fledging: 14-18 days; female and male feed young

Migration: complete migrator, to southwestern states, non-migrator in most of New Mexico

Food: insects

Compare: Slightly larger than Canyon Wren (pg. 105), which has a much larger and down-curved bill and is mostly chestnut brown. Slightly larger than the House Wren (pg. 85), which lacks Rock Wren's white speckles on back.

Stan's Notes: Consistently uses open sunny piles of broken rocks (scree) and rock debris at cliff bases (talus slopes) for nesting. Often builds a small runway of flat stones leading up to the nest, which is usually in a rock crevice. Lives in close association with Canyon Wrens, which use steep-sided canyons for nesting. Known to also nest on prairies, where it uses dirt banks instead of rock piles. The female does most of the incubating, with the male feeding female during incubation.

male

female

HOUSE SPARROW
Passer domesticus

Size: 6" (15 cm)

Male: Medium sparrow-like bird with large black spot on throat extending down to the chest. Brown back and single white wing bars. A gray belly and crown.

Female: slightly smaller than the male, light brown, lacks the throat patch and single wing bars

Juvenile: similar to female

Nest: domed cup nest, within cavity; female and male build; 2-3 broods per year

Eggs: 4-6; white with brown markings

Incubation: 10-12 days; female incubates

Fledging: 14-17 days; female and male feed young

Migration: non-migrator; moves around to find food

Food: seeds, insects, fruit; comes to seed feeders

Compare: Lacks the rusty crown of Chipping Sparrow (pg. 91). Look for male House Sparrow's black bib. Female has a clear breast and no marking on head (cap).

Stan's Notes: One of the first bird songs heard in cities in spring. Familiar city bird, nearly always in small flocks. Introduced from Europe to Central Park, New York, in 1850. Now found throughout North America. These birds are not really sparrows, but members of the Weaver Finch family, characterized by their large, oversized domed nests. Constructs a nest containing scraps of plastic, paper and whatever else is available. An aggressive bird that will kill the young of other birds in order to take over a cavity.

female

male pg. 303

YEAR-ROUND
WINTER

CASSIN'S FINCH
Carpodacus cassinii

Size: 6½" (16 cm)

Female: Brown-to-gray finch with fine black streaks on back and wings. Heavily streaked white chest and belly.

Male: light wash of crimson red, especially bright red crown, brown streaks on the back and wings, white belly

Juvenile: similar to female

Nest: cup; female builds; 1-2 broods per year

Eggs: 3-5; white without markings

Incubation: 12-14 days; female incubates

Fledging: 14-18 days; female and male feed young

Migration: partial migrator to non-migrator; will move around to find food

Food: seeds, insects, fruits, berries; will visit seed feeders

Compare: The female House Finch (pg. 89) is similar, but has a gray belly that is not as streaked.

Stan's Notes: This is a mountain finch of coniferous forests. Usually forages for seeds on the ground, but eats evergreen buds and aspen and willow catkins. Breeds in May. A colony nester, depending on the regional source of food. The more food available, the larger the colony. Male sings a rapid warble, often imitating other birds such as jays, tanagers and grosbeaks. A cowbird host.

SUMMER

LARK SPARROW
Chondestes grammacus

Size: 6½" (16 cm)

Male: All-brown bird with unique rust red, white and black head pattern. White breast with a central black spot. Gray rump and white edges to gray tail, as seen in flight.

Female: same as male

Juvenile: similar to adult, no rust red on head

Nest: cup, on the ground; female builds; 1 brood per year

Eggs: 3-6; pale white with brown markings

Incubation: 10-12 days; male and female incubate

Fledging: 10-12 days; female and male feed young

Migration: complete, coastal Mexico, Central America

Food: seeds, insects

Compare: The White-throated Sparrow (pg. 115) and the White-crowned Sparrow (pg. 117) both lack the Lark Sparrow's rust red pattern on the head and central spot on a white chest. Larger than the Chipping Sparrow (pg. 91), which has a similar rusty color on head, but lacks Lark's white chest and central spot.

Stan's Notes: One of the larger sparrow species and one of the best songsters, also well known for its courtship strutting, chasing and lark-like flight pattern (rapid wing beats with tail spread). A bird of open fields, pastures and prairies, found almost anywhere there are no mountains. Very common during migration, when large flocks congregate. Uses nest for several years if first brood is successful.

113

white-striped

tan-striped

WHITE-THROATED SPARROW
Zonotrichia albicollis

MIGRATION
WINTER

Size: 6-7" (15-18 cm)

Male: A brown bird with gray tan chest and belly. Small yellow spot between the eyes (lore). Distinctive white or tan throat patch. White or tan stripes alternate with black stripes on crown. Color of the throat patch and crown stripes match.

Female: same as male

Juvenile: similar to adult, gray throat and eyebrows with heavily streaked chest

Nest: cup; female builds; 1 brood per year

Eggs: 4-6; color varies from greenish to bluish to creamy white with red brown markings

Incubation: 11-14 days; female incubates

Fledging: 10-12 days; female and male feed young

Migration: complete, to New Mexico and Mexico

Food: insects, seeds, fruit; visits ground feeders

Compare: White-crowned Sparrow (pg. 117) lacks the throat patch and yellow lore. Lark Sparrow (pg. 113) has a rust red pattern on the head and central black spot on a white chest.

Stan's Notes: Two color variations (polymorphic). Studies indicate that white-striped adults tend to mate with tan-striped birds. No indication why. Known for its wonderful song. Sings all year, even at night. Both white- and tan-striped males sing with white-striped females, but tan-striped females do not sing. Often associated with other sparrows in winter. More abundant during migration, when it visits ground feeders. Builds nest on the ground under small trees.

juvenile

WHITE-CROWNED SPARROW
Zonotrichia leucophrys

Size: 6½-7½" (16-19 cm)

Male: A brown sparrow with a gray breast and a black-and-white striped crown. Small, thin pink bill.

Female: same as male

Juvenile: similar to adult, with brown stripes on the head instead of white

Nest: cup; female builds; 2 broods per year

Eggs: 3-5; color varies from greenish to bluish to whitish with red brown markings

Incubation: 11-14 days; female incubates

Fledging: 8-12 days; male and female feed young

Migration: complete migrator, to southwestern states, Mexico, non-migrator in northern parts of New Mexico

Food: insects, seeds, berries; visits ground feeders

Compare: The White-throated Sparrow (pg. 115) has a white or tan throat patch, and yellow spot between eyes and bill. The Lark Sparrow (pg. 113) has a rust red pattern on the head.

Stan's Notes: A year-round resident in a small portion of northern New Mexico and winter visitor throughout. Usually seen in groups of up to 20 during migration, when it can be seen feeding beneath seed feeders. A ground feeder, scratching backward with both feet at the same time. Male sparrows arrive before females and establish territories by singing from perches. Nesting starts in May. Male takes most of the responsibility of raising the young while female starts the second brood. Only 9-12 days separate broods.

FOX SPARROW
Passerella iliaca

MIGRATION
WINTER

Size: 7" (18 cm)

Male: Plump brown sparrow with a gray head, back and rump. White chest and belly with rusty brown streaks. Rusty tail and wings.

Female: same as male

Juvenile: same as adult

Nest: cup; female builds; 2 broods per year

Eggs: 2-4; pale green with reddish markings

Incubation: 12-14 days; female incubates

Fledging: 10-11 days; female and male feed young

Migration: complete, to southern New Mexico

Food: seeds, insects; comes to feeders

Compare: The Spotted Towhee (pg. 9) is found in a similar habitat, but male Spotted Towhee has a black head.

Stan's Notes: One of the largest sparrows. Several color variations, depending upon the part of the country. Fox Sparrows in western states have gray heads and backs. Usually seen alone or in small groups, often beneath seed feeders looking for seeds and insects. Scratches like a chicken with both feet at the same time to find food. Builds a cup nest in brush on the ground and along forest edges. The common name "Sparrow" comes from the Anglo-Saxon word *spearwa*, meaning "flutterer," as applies to any small bird. "Fox" refers to the bird's rusty color.

male pg. 71

female

BLUE GROSBEAK
Passerina caerulea

Size: 7" (18 cm)

Female: Overall brown with darker wings and tail. Two tan wing bars. Large gray-to-silver bill.

Male: blue bird with 2 chestnut wing bars, a large gray-to-silver bill, black around base of bill

Juvenile: similar to female

Nest: cup; female builds; 1-2 broods per year

Eggs: 3-6; pale blue without markings

Incubation: 11-12 days; female incubates

Fledging: 9-10 days; female and male feed young

Migration: complete, to Mexico and Central America

Food: insects, seeds; will come to seed feeders

Compare: Female Lazuli Bunting (pg. 99) and Indigo Bunting (pg. 97) are similar, but lack tan wing bars and are a lighter color overall.

Stan's Notes: This bird returns to New Mexico by early May. It has expanded northward with overall populations increasing over the past 30-40 years. A bird of semi-open habitats such as overgrown fields, riversides, woodland edges and fencerows. Frequently seen twitching and spreading its tail. First-year males show only some blue, obtaining the full complement of blue feathers in the second winter. Visits seed feeders.

YEAR-ROUND

HORNED LARK
Eremophila alpestris

Size: 7-8" (18-20 cm)

Male: A sleek tan-to-brown bird. Black necklace with a yellow chin and black bill. Two tiny "horns" on the top of head can be difficult to see. A dark tail with white outer feathers, noticeable in flight.

Female: duller than male, "horns" less noticeable

Juvenile: lacks the black markings and yellow chin, doesn't form "horns" until second year

Nest: ground; female builds; 2-3 broods per year

Eggs: 3-4; gray with brown markings

Incubation: 11-12 days; female incubates

Fledging: 9-12 days; female and male feed young

Migration: non-migrator in New Mexico

Food: seeds, insects

Compare: Smaller than Meadowlark (pg. 339), which shares the black necklace and yellow chin. Look for the black marks in front of eyes.

Stan's Notes: The only true lark native to North America. A year-round resident, moving about in winter to find food. Horned Larks are birds of open ground. Common in rural areas, frequently seen in large flocks. Population increased in North America over the past 100 years due to land clearing for farming. May have up to three broods per year because they get such an early start. Male performs a fluttering courtship flight high in the air while singing a high-pitched song. Female performs a fluttering distraction display if nest is disturbed. Can renest about a week after brood fledges. The name "Lark" comes from the Middle English word *laverock*, or "a lark."

1 year old

Bohemian
Waxwing

CEDAR WAXWING
Bombycilla cedrorum

Size: 7½" (19 cm)

Male: Very sleek-looking gray-to-brown bird with pointed crest, light yellow belly and bandit-like black mask. Tip of tail is bright yellow and the tips of wings look as if they have been dipped in red wax.

Female: same as male

Juvenile: grayish with a heavily streaked chest, lacks red wing tips, black mask and sleek look

Nest: cup; female and male construct; 1 brood per year, occasionally 2

Eggs: 4-6; pale blue with brown markings

Incubation: 10-12 days; female incubates

Fledging: 14-18 days; female and male feed young

Migration: complete to partial migrator; moves to New Mexico to find food

Food: cedar cones, fruit, insects

Compare: Similar to its larger, less common cousin, the Bohemian Waxwing (see inset), which has white on wings and rust under the tail.

Stan's Notes: The name is derived from its red wax-like wing tips and preference for eating small blueberry-like cones of the cedar. Mostly seen in flocks, moving from area to area, looking for berries. Wanders in winter to find available food supplies. During summer, before berries are abundant, it feeds on insects. Spends most of its time at the tops of tall trees. Listen for the very high-pitched "sreee" whistling sounds it constantly makes. Obtains mask after first year and red wing tips after second year. Doesn't nest in New Mexico.

male pg. 3

female

BROWN-HEADED COWBIRD
Molothrus ater

YEAR-ROUND
SUMMER

Size: 7½" (19 cm)

Female: Dull brown bird with no obvious markings. Pointed, sharp gray bill.

Male: glossy black bird, chocolate brown head

Juvenile: similar to female, only dull gray color and a streaked chest

Nest: no nest; lays eggs in nests of other birds

Eggs: 5-7; white with brown markings

Incubation: 10-13 days; host bird incubates eggs

Fledging: 10-11 days; host birds feed young

Migration: non-migrator to partial in New Mexico

Food: insects, seeds; will come to seed feeders

Compare: Female Red-winged Blackbird (pg. 137) is slightly larger and has white eyebrows and a streaked chest. European Starling (pg. 5) has speckles and a shorter tail.

Stan's Notes: A member of the blackbird family. Of approximately 750 species of parasitic birds worldwide, this is the only parasitic bird in the state, laying eggs in host birds' nests, leaving others to raise its young. Cowbirds are known to have laid eggs in nests of over 200 species of birds. Some birds reject cowbird eggs, but most incubate them and raise the young, even to the exclusion of their own. Look for warblers and other birds feeding young birds twice their own size. At one time cowbirds followed bison to feed on insects attracted to the animals.

SUMMER

COMMON POORWILL
Phalaenoptilus nuttallii

Size: 7¾" (19.5 cm)

Male: A small all-brown bird with a short tail and short rounded wings. White necklace and tip of tail.

Female: same as male

Juvenile: similar to adult

Nest: no nest; female scrapes a depression in the gravel; 1 brood per year

Eggs: 1-2; pale white with brown markings

Incubation: unknown days; incubation unknown

Fledging: unknown days; female and male feed young

Migration: complete migrator, to Mexico, Central and South America

Food: insects

Compare: The Common Nighthawk (pg. 143) is very similar, but larger, with a long narrow tail and white band across each wing, as seen in flight.

Stan's Notes: Not much is known about this secretive species. It nests in open places below 8,000-foot (2,450 m) elevations. The excellent camouflage coloring and habit of not flushing off its nest or roosting make this bird hard to find and study. A nocturnal bird, usually only seen flying at dusk, flitting its wings more like a moth than a bird. Feeds on flying insects and drinks from the surface of water while in flight. Often easier to hear than to see at night. Gives a soft, low "poor-will" whistle, which accounts for the common name. Some that don't migrate have been found in a hibernation-like state (torpor).

winter

breeding

SPOTTED SANDPIPER
Actitis macularia

MIGRATION
SUMMER
WINTER

Size: 8" (20 cm)

Male: Olive brown back. Long bill and long dull yellow legs. White line over eyes. Breeding plumage has black spots on a white chest and belly. Winter has a clear chest and belly.

Female: same as male

Juvenile: similar to winter adult, with a darker bill

Nest: ground; female and male build; 2 broods per year

Eggs: 3-4; brownish with brown markings

Incubation: 20-24 days; male incubates

Fledging: 17-21 days; male feeds young

Migration: complete, to southern New Mexico, Mexico, Central and South America

Food: aquatic insects

Compare: The Killdeer (pg. 151) has 2 black bands around neck. Look for Spotted Sandpiper to bob its tail up and down while standing. Look for the breeding Spotted Sandpiper's black spots extending from chest to belly.

Stan's Notes: One of the few sandpipers in New Mexico. Also one of the few shorebirds that will dive underwater if pursued. Able to fly straight up out of water. Flies with wings held in a cup-like arc, rarely lifting them above a horizontal plane. Constantly bobs its tail while standing and walks as if delicately balanced. Female mates with multiple males and lays eggs in up to five different nests. Male incubates and cares for young. Dramatic plumage change from breeding to winter. Lacks black spots on chest and belly in winter.

male pg. 297

female

BLACK-HEADED GROSBEAK
Pheucticus melanocephalus

Size: 8" (20 cm)

Female: Appears like an overgrown sparrow. Overall brown with a lighter breast and belly. Large two-toned bill. Prominent white eyebrows. Yellow wing linings, as seen in flight.

Male: burnt orange chest, neck and rump, black head, tail and wings with irregular-shaped white wing patches, large bill with upper bill darker than lower

Juvenile: similar to adult of the same sex

Nest: cup; female builds; 1 brood per year

Eggs: 3-4; pale green or bluish, brown markings

Incubation: 11-13 days; female and male incubate

Fledging: 11-13 days; female and male feed young

Migration: complete, to Mexico, Central America and South America

Food: seeds, insects, fruit; comes to seed feeders

Compare: Female House Finch (pg. 89) is smaller, has more streaking on the chest and bill isn't as large. Look for the unusual bicolored bill of the female Black-headed Grosbeak.

Stan's Notes: A cosmopolitan bird that nests in a wide variety of habitats, seeming to prefer the foothills slightly more than other places. Both males and females sing and aggressively defend their nests against intruders. Song is very similar to the American Robin's and Western Tanager's, making it hard to tell them apart by song. Populations are increasing in New Mexico and across the U.S.

CACTUS WREN
Campylorhynchus brunneicapillus

Size: 8½" (22 cm)

Male: A large round-bodied wren with a long tail and a large, slightly downward curving bill. Bold white eyebrows and a chestnut brown crown. Many dark spots on upper breast to throat, often forming a central dark patch.

Female: same as male

Juvenile: similar to adult, shorter bill, lacks a spotty dark patch on breast

Nest: covered cup, domed or ball-shaped; female and male build; 2-3 broods per year

Eggs: 3-4; pale white to pink with brown marks

Incubation: 14-16 days; female incubates

Fledging: 19-23 days; female and male feed young

Migration: non-migrator

Food: insects, fruit, seeds; comes to seed feeders and water elements

Compare: Sage Thrasher (pg. 235) is gray and lacks a down-curving bill. Curve-billed Thrasher (pg. 251) has a longer bill. Look for Cactus Wren's bold white eyebrows to help identify.

Stan's Notes: Our largest wren. Backyard bird with a loud "krr-krr-krr-krr-krr" or "cha-cha-cha-cha." Male crouches, extends wings, fans tail and growls to female during courtship. Pairs stay together all year, defending territory. Builds a large nest usually in cholla or cactus, lining the chamber with grasses and feathers. Male builds another nest while female incubates first clutch of eggs. After the second brood fledges, roosts in nest during non-breeding season.

male pg. 11

female

YEAR-ROUND

RED-WINGED BLACKBIRD
Agelaius phoeniceus

Size: 8½" (22 cm)

Female: Heavily streaked brown bird with a pointed brown bill and white eyebrows.

Male: jet black bird with red and yellow patches on upper wings, pointed black bill

Juvenile: same as female

Nest: cup; female builds; 2-3 broods per year

Eggs: 3-4; bluish green with brown markings

Incubation: 10-12 days; female incubates

Fledging: 11-14 days; female and male feed young

Migration: non-migrator to partial migrator

Food: seeds, insects; will come to seed feeders

Compare: Female Brewer's Blackbird (pg. 139) and female Yellow-headed Blackbird (pg. 147) are larger. Female Brown-headed Cowbird (pg. 127) is smaller. All three species lack white eyebrows and heavily streaked chest of the female Red-winged Blackbird.

Stan's Notes: One of the most widespread and numerous birds in the state. It is a sure sign of spring when the Red-winged Blackbirds return to the marshes. Flocks of up to 100,000 birds have been reported. Males return before the females and defend territories by singing from tops of surrounding vegetation. Males repeat call from the tops of cattails while showing off their red and yellow wing bars (epaulets). Females choose mate and usually will nest over shallow water in thick stands of cattails. Red-wingeds feed mostly on seeds in fall and spring, switching to insects during summer.

137

male pg. 13

female

BREWER'S BLACKBIRD
Euphagus cyanocephalus

Size: 9" (22.5 cm)

Female: An overall grayish brown bird. Legs and bill nearly black. While most have dark eyes, some have bright white or pale yellow eyes.

Male: glossy black, shining green in direct light, head purplish, white or pale yellow eyes

Juvenile: similar to female

Nest: cup; female builds; 1-2 broods per year

Eggs: 4-6; gray with brown markings

Incubation: 12-14 days; female incubates

Fledging: 13-14 days; female and male feed young

Migration: non-migrator to partial in New Mexico; will move around to find food

Food: insects, seeds, fruit

Compare: Larger in size and darker in color than the female Brown-headed Cowbird (pg. 127). Female Red-winged Blackbird (pg. 137) is similar in size, but has a heavily streaked chest and prominent white eyebrows.

Stan's Notes: Often in fields and open places such as wet pastures and mountain meadows up to 10,000 feet (3,050 m). Male and some females are easily identified by their bright, nearly white eyes. A cowbird host. Usually nests in a shrub, small tree or on ground. Prefers to nest in small colonies, up to 20 pairs. Doesn't get along with Common Grackles; often driven out of nest area by expansion of grackles. Gathers in large flocks with cowbirds, Red-wingeds and other blackbirds to migrate. Expanding its range in North America.

CANYON TOWHEE
Pipilo fuscus

Size: 9" (22.5 cm)

Male: Dull brown to dark gray with a salmon pink lower belly and base of tail. Light tan throat. Distinctive necklace of dark spots. A central dark spot on the chest. Rusty cap. Small tan patch "lore" in front of each eye. Tail darker than rest of body. Small gray bill.

Female: same as male

Juvenile: similar to adult, but has streaking on breast and necklace is not as well defined

Nest: cup; female builds; 1 brood per year

Eggs: 3-4; pale blue or white with brown marks

Incubation: 11-13 days; female incubates

Fledging: 12-13 days; female and male feed young

Migration: non-migrator

Food: seeds, insects, fruit; visits ground feeders

Compare: The Green-tailed Towhee (pg. 283) has a brighter rusty cap and bright white throat.

Stan's Notes: Usually found in desert scrub near water. Lines its bulky nest of stems and twigs with fine plant material. Often runs across the ground with head down when disturbed to quickly get to cover of shrubs or cacti. Male droops wings and quivers while "squealing" in front of the female during courtship. Comes to seeds spread on the ground or platform feeders that offer millet and sunflower seeds. Reportedly drinks dew from vegetation. Young are fed insects. Formerly called Brown Towhee.

female

male

COMMON NIGHTHAWK
Chordeiles minor

Size: 9" (22.5 cm)

Male: A camouflaged brown and white bird with white chin. A distinctive white band across wings and the tail, seen only in flight.

Female: similar to male, but with tan chin, lacks the white tail band

Juvenile: similar to female

Nest: no nest; lays eggs on the ground, usually on rocks, or on rooftop; 1 brood per year

Eggs: 2; cream with lavender markings

Incubation: 19-20 days; female and male incubate

Fledging: 20-21 days; female and male feed young

Migration: complete, to South America

Food: insects caught in air

Compare: Common Poorwill (pg. 129) is similar, but smaller and has a shorter tail. Look for the obvious white wing band of the Common Nighthawk in flight and the characteristic flap-flap-flap-glide flight pattern.

Stan's Notes: Usually only seen flying at dusk or after sunset, but not uncommon for it to be sitting on a fence post, sleeping during the day. A very noisy bird, repeating a "peenting" call during flight. Alternates slow wing beats with bursts of quick wing beats. Prolific insect eater. Prefers gravel rooftops for nesting in cities and nests on the ground in country. Male's distinctive springtime mating ritual is a steep diving flight terminated with a loud popping noise. One of the first birds to migrate each fall, starting in August.

SUMMER

BURROWING OWL
Athene cunicularia

Size: 9½" (24 cm); up to 21-inch wingspan

Male: A brown owl with bold white spots, white belly and very long legs. Yellow eyes.

Female: same as male

Juvenile: same as adult, but belly is brown

Nest: cavity, former underground mammal den; female and male line den; 1 brood per year

Eggs: 6-11; white without markings

Incubation: 21-28 days; female incubates

Fledging: 25-28 days; female and male feed young

Migration: complete, to Mexico and Central America

Food: insects, mammals, lizards, birds

Compare: Western Screech-Owl (pg. 237) is slightly smaller and has ear tufts. Burrowing Owl is less than half the size of Great Horned Owl (pg. 193), which has feather tuft "horns." Burrowing spends most of its time on the ground unlike tree-loving Great Horned.

Stan's Notes: An owl of fields, open backyards, golf courses and airports. Nests in small family units or in small colonies. Takes over the underground dens of mammals, occasionally widening its den by kicking dirt backward. Lines den with cow pies, horse dung, grass and feathers. Some people have had success attracting these owls to their backyards by creating artificial dens. Often seen in the day, standing or sleeping around den entrance. Male brings food to incubating female, often moving family to a new den when young are just a few weeks old. Will bob head up and down while doing deep knee bends when agitated or threatened.

male pg. 15

female

YELLOW-HEADED BLACKBIRD
Xanthocephalus xanthocephalus

MIGRATION
SUMMER
WINTER

Size: 9-11" (22.5-28 cm)

Female: A large brown bird with a dull yellow head and chest. Slightly smaller than male.

Male: black bird with a lemon yellow head, chest and nape of neck, black mask and gray bill, white wing patches

Juvenile: similar to female

Nest: cup; female builds; 2 broods per year

Eggs: 3-5; greenish white with brown markings

Incubation: 11-13 days; female incubates

Fledging: 9-12 days; female feeds young

Migration: complete, to southern New Mexico, Mexico

Food: insects, seeds; will come to ground feeders

Compare: Larger than female Red-winged Blackbird (pg. 137), which has white eyebrows and streaked chest.

Stan's Notes: Usually heard before seen, Yellow-headed Blackbird has a low, hoarse, raspy or metallic call. Nests in deep water marshes unlike its cousin, the Red-winged Blackbird, which prefers shallow water. The male gives an impressive mating display, flying with head drooped and feet and tail pointing down while steadily beating its wings. The female incubates alone and feeds 3-5 young. Young keep low and out of sight for as many as three weeks before starting to fly. Migrates in flocks of up to 200 with other blackbirds. Flocks made up mainly of males return first in early April; females return later. Most colonies consist of 20-100 nests.

male

female

AMERICAN KESTREL
Falco sparverius

Size: 10-12" (25-30 cm); up to 2-foot wingspan

Male: Rusty brown back and tail. A white breast with dark spots. Double black vertical lines on white face. Blue gray wings. Distinctive wide black band with a white edge on tip of rusty tail.

Female: similar to male, but slightly larger, has rusty brown wings and dark bands on tail

Juvenile: same as adult of the same sex

Nest: cavity; doesn't build a nest within; 1 brood per year

Eggs: 4-5; white with brown markings

Incubation: 29-31 days; male and female incubate

Fledging: 30-31 days; female and male feed young

Migration: non-migrator in New Mexico

Food: insects, small mammals and birds, reptiles

Compare: Similar to other falcons. Look for 2 vertical black stripes on the Kestrel's face. No other small bird of prey has a rusty back and tail.

Stan's Notes: A falcon that was once called Sparrow Hawk due to its small size. Could be called Grasshopper Hawk because it eats many grasshoppers. Can see ultraviolet light; this ability helps it locate mice and other small mammals by their urine, which glows bright yellow in ultraviolet light. Hovers near roads before diving for prey. Adapts quickly to a wooden nest box. Has pointed swept-back wings, seen in flight. Perches nearly upright. Unusual raptor in that males and females have quite different markings. Watch for them to pump their tails up and down after landing on perches.

KILLDEER
Charadrius vociferus

YEAR-ROUND

Size: 11" (28 cm)

Male: An upland shorebird that has 2 black bands around the neck like a necklace. A brown back and white belly. Bright reddish orange rump, visible in flight.

Female: same as male

Juvenile: similar to adult, with 1 neck band

Nest: ground; male builds; 2 broods per year

Eggs: 3-5; tan with brown markings

Incubation: 24-28 days; male and female incubate

Fledging: 25 days; male and female lead their young to food

Migration: non-migrator in New Mexico

Food: insects

Compare: The Spotted Sandpiper (pg. 131) is found around water and lacks the 2 neck bands of the Killdeer.

Stan's Notes: The only shorebird with two black neck bands. It is known for its broken wing impression, which draws intruders away from nest. Once clear of the nest, the Killdeer takes flight. Nests are only a slight depression in a gravel area, often very difficult to see. Young look like yellow cotton balls on stilts when first hatched, but quickly molt to appear similar to parents. Able to follow parents and peck for insects soon after birth. Is technically classified as a shorebird, but doesn't live at the shore. Often found in vacant fields or along railroads. Has a very distinctive "kill-deer" call.

red-shafted
male

yellow-shafted
female

red-shafted
female

yellow-shafted
male

NORTHERN FLICKER
Colaptes auratus

Size: 12" (30 cm)

Male: Brown and black woodpecker with a large white rump patch visible only when flying. Black necklace above a speckled chest. Gray head with a brown cap. Red mustache.

Female: same as male, but lacks the red mustache

Juvenile: same as adult of the same sex

Nest: cavity; female and male excavate; 1 brood per year

Eggs: 5-8; white without markings

Incubation: 11-14 days; female and male incubate

Fledging: 25-28 days; female and male feed young

Migration: complete to non-migrator in New Mexico

Food: insects, especially ants and beetles

Compare: This is the only brown-backed woodpecker in New Mexico. Look for its speckled chest and gray head to help identify.

Stan's Notes: The flicker is the only woodpecker to regularly feed on the ground, preferring ants and beetles. Produces antacid saliva to neutralize the acidic defense of ants. Male usually selects a nest site, taking up to 12 days to excavate. Some have been successful attracting flickers to nest boxes stuffed with sawdust. Red-shafted males have red mustaches, while yellow-shafted males have black mustaches. Yellow-shafteds have golden yellow wing linings and tails. Both varieties undulate deeply during flight while giving loud "wacka-wacka" calls. Hybrids between varieties occur in the Great Plains, where the ranges overlap. Map reflects the combined range.

153

MOURNING DOVE
Zenaida macroura

Size: 12" (30 cm)

Male: Smooth fawn-colored dove with gray patch on the head. Iridescent pink, green around neck. A single black spot behind and below eyes. Black spots on wings and tail. Pointed wedge-shaped tail with white edges.

Female: similar to male, lacking iridescent pink and green neck feathers

Juvenile: spotted and streaked

Nest: platform; female and male build; 2 broods per year

Eggs: 2; white without markings

Incubation: 13-14 days; male and female incubate, male incubates during the day, female at night

Fledging: 12-14 days; female and male feed young

Migration: non-migrator to partial migrator; will move around to find food

Food: seeds; will visit seed and ground feeders

Compare: Smaller than Rock Pigeon (pg. 261), lacking its wide range of color combinations.

Stan's Notes: Name comes from its mournful cooing. A ground feeder, bobbing its head as it walks. One of the few birds to drink without lifting its head, same as Rock Pigeon. Parents feed young a regurgitated liquid called crop-milk for the first few days of life. Flimsy platform nest of twigs often falls apart during a storm. Wind rushing through wing feathers during flight creates a characteristic whistling sound.

winter

breeding

PIED-BILLED GREBE
Podilymbus podiceps

Size: 13" (33 cm)

Male: Small brown water bird with a black chin and black ring around a thick, chicken-like ivory bill. Puffy white patch under the tail. Has an unmarked brown bill during winter (September to February).

Female: same as male

Juvenile: paler than adult, with white spots and gray chest, belly and bill

Nest: floating platform; female and male build; 1 brood per year

Eggs: 5-7; bluish white without markings

Incubation: 22-24 days; female and male incubate

Fledging: 22-24 days; female and male feed young

Migration: non-migrator in New Mexico

Food: crayfish, aquatic insects, fish

Compare: Look for a puffy white patch under the tail and thick, chicken-like bill to help identify.

Stan's Notes: Common resident grebe, often seen diving for food. Slowly sinks like a submarine if disturbed. Sinks without diving by quickly compressing feathers to force air out. Was called Hell-diver because of the length of time it can stay submerged. Can surface far from where it went under. Very sensitive to pollution. Adapted well to life on water, with short wings, lobed toes, and legs set close to rear of body. While swimming is easy, it is very awkward on land. Builds nest on a floating mat in water. "Grebe" probably came from the Old English *krib*, meaning "crest," a reference to the crested head plumes of many grebes, especially during breeding season.

male pg. 21

female

GREAT-TAILED GRACKLE
Quiscalus mexicanus

YEAR-ROUND

Size: 15" (38 cm), female
18" (45 cm), male

Female: An overall brown bird with a gray-to-brown belly. Light brown-to-white eyes, eyebrows, throat and upper portion of chest.

Male: all-black bird with iridescent purple sheen on head and back, exceptionally long tail, bright yellow eyes

Juvenile: similar to female

Nest: cup; female builds; 1-2 broods per year

Eggs: 3-5; greenish blue with brown markings

Incubation: 12-14 days; female incubates

Fledging: 21-23 days; female feeds young

Migration: non-migrator to partial in New Mexico; will move around to find food

Food: insects, fruit, seeds; comes to seed feeders

Compare: Larger than the female Brewer's Blackbird (pg. 139), with a much lighter brown chest and distinct light brown eyebrows.

Stan's Notes: This is our largest grackle. It was once considered a subspecies of the Boat-tailed Grackle, which occurs along the East coast and Florida. A bird that prefers to nest near water in an open habitat. A colony nester, males do not participate in nest building, incubation or raising of young. Males rarely fight, but females will squabble over nest sites and materials. Several females mate with one male. They are expanding northward, moving into northern states. Western populations tend to be larger than the eastern. Song varies from population to population.

male

female

BLUE-WINGED TEAL
Anas discors

YEAR-ROUND
MIGRATION
SUMMER

Size: 15-16" (38-40 cm)

Male: Small, plain-looking brown duck speckled with black. A gray head with a large white crescent-shaped mark at base of bill. Black tail with small white patch. Blue wing patch (speculum) usually seen only in flight.

Female: duller version of male, lacks facial crescent mark and white patch on tail, showing only slight white at base of bill

Juvenile: same as female

Nest: ground; female builds; 1 brood per year

Eggs: 8-11; creamy white

Incubation: 23-27 days; female incubates

Fledging: 35-44 days; female feeds young

Migration: complete, to southern New Mexico, Mexico and Central America

Food: aquatic plants, seeds, aquatic insects

Compare: Male Blue-winged has a distinct white face marking. The female Blue-winged is smaller than the female Mallard (pg. 171).

Stan's Notes: One of the smallest ducks in North America. An early migrator in the state. Most breeding birds here leave before other, more northern ducks pass through in fall. Nests some distance from water. Female performs a distraction display to protect her nest and young. Male leaves the female near the end of incubation. Planting crops and cultivating to pond edges have caused the population to decline in many parts of its range. Widespread nesting, breeding as far north as Alaska. One of the longest distance migrating ducks.

male pg. 47

female

LESSER SCAUP
Aythya affinis

Size: 16-17" (40-43 cm)

Female: Overall brown duck with dull white patch at base of light gray bill. Yellow eyes.

Male: white and gray, the chest and head appear nearly black but head appears purple with green highlights in direct sun, yellow eyes

Juvenile: same as female

Nest: ground; female builds; 1 brood per year

Eggs: 8-14; olive buff without markings

Incubation: 22-28 days; female incubates

Fledging: 45-50 days; female teaches young to feed

Migration: complete, to southwestern states, Mexico, Central America, northern South America

Food: aquatic plants and insects

Compare: Similar size as the female Ring-necked Duck (pg. 165), but lacking the white ring around the bill. Look for the white patch at the base of the bill to help identify the female Lesser Scaup. Male Blue-winged Teal (pg. 161) is smaller, with a crescent-shaped white mark near the base of bill.

Stan's Notes: Common diving duck. Often in large flocks on lakes, ponds and sewage lagoons. Submerges to feed on bottom of lakes (unlike dabbling ducks, which tip forward to reach bottom). Note the bold white stripe under wings when in flight. Male leaves female when she starts to incubate her eggs. Quantity of eggs (clutch size) increases with age of female. Interesting baby-sitting arrangement in which groups of young (crèches) are tended by 1-3 adult females.

male pg. 49

female

MIGRATION
WINTER

RING-NECKED DUCK
Aythya collaris

Size: 17" (43 cm)

Female: Mainly brown back with light brown sides, a gray face and dark brown crown. White eye-ring extends into a line behind eyes. A white ring around a light blue bill. Top of head is peaked.

Male: black head, breast and back, sides are gray to nearly white, a bold white ring around a light blue bill and second ring at the base of bill, top of head is peaked

Juvenile: similar to female

Nest: ground; female builds; 1 brood per year

Eggs: 8-10; olive gray to brown without markings

Incubation: 26-27 days; female incubates

Fledging: 49-56 days; female teaches young to feed

Migration: complete migrator, to southwestern states, Mexico and Central America

Food: aquatic plants and insects

Compare: Female Lesser Scaup (pg. 163) is similar in size. Look for female Ring-necked Duck's white ring around the bill.

Stan's Notes: A common winter duck in New Mexico. Usually is seen in larger freshwater lakes. A diving duck, watch for it to dive underwater to forage for food. Takes to flight by springing up off water. Was named "Ring-necked" because of the cinnamon collar (nearly impossible to see in the field). Also called Ring-billed Duck due to the white ring on its bill, and Blue Bill by duck hunters.

male pg. 307

female

REDHEAD
Aythya americana

YEAR-ROUND
WINTER

Size: 19" (48 cm)

Female: Plain, soft brown duck with gray-to-white wing linings. Top of head is rounded. Two-toned bill, gray with a black tip.

Male: rich red head and neck with a black breast and tail, gray sides, smoky gray wings and back, tricolored bill with a light blue base, white ring and black tip

Juvenile: similar to female

Nest: cup; female builds; 1 brood per year

Eggs: 9-14; pale white without markings

Incubation: 24-28 days; female and male incubate

Fledging: 56-73 days; female shows the young what to eat

Migration: complete migrator, to southwestern states, Mexico and Central America

Food: seeds, aquatic plants, insects

Compare: The female Northern Shoveler (pg. 177) is a lighter brown with an exceptionally large shovel-shaped bill.

Stan's Notes: A duck of permanent large bodies of water. Forages along the shoreline, feeding on seeds, aquatic plants and insects. Usually builds nest directly on surface of water, using large mats of vegetation. Female lays up to 75 percent of its eggs in the nests of other Redheads and several other duck species. Nests primarily in the Prairie Pothole region of the northern Great Plains. The overall populations seem to be increasing at about 2-3 percent each year.

female

male pg. 53

COMMON GOLDENEYE
Bucephala clangula

Size:	18½-20" (47-50 cm)
Female:	A brown and gray duck with a large dark brown head and gray body. White collar. Bright golden eyes. Yellow-tipped dark bill.
Male:	mostly white duck with a black back and a large, puffy green head, large white spot in front of each bright golden eye, dark bill
Juvenile:	same as female, but has a dark bill
Nest:	cavity; female lines old woodpecker cavity; 1 brood per year
Eggs:	8-10; light green without markings
Incubation:	28-32 days; female incubates
Fledging:	56-59 days; female leads young to food
Migration:	complete, to southwestern states, Mexico
Food:	aquatic plants, insects
Compare:	Female Lesser Scaup (pg. 163) is similar but smaller. Similar size as the female Redhead (pg. 167), which is uniformly light brown, lacking the gray body of female Goldeneye. Look for the dark brown head and white collar of the female Common Goldeneye.

Stan's Notes: Known for its loud whistling, produced by its wings in flight. In late winter and early spring, male often attracts female through elaborate displays, throwing its head backward while it utters a single raspy note. Female will lay eggs in other goldeneye nests, which results in some mothers incubating up to 30 eggs. Received the common name from its obvious bright golden eyes. Winters in New Mexico where it finds open water.

male pg. 287

female

Mexican

MALLARD
Anas platyrhynchos

Size: 19-21" (48-53 cm)

Female: Brown duck with an orange and black bill and blue and white wing mark (speculum).

Male: large, bulbous green head, white necklace, rust brown or chestnut chest, combination of gray and white on the sides, yellow bill, orange legs and feet

Juvenile: same as female, but with a yellow bill

Nest: ground; female builds; 1 brood per year

Eggs: 7-10; greenish to whitish, unmarked

Incubation: 26-30 days; female incubates

Fledging: 42-52 days; female leads young to food

Migration: partial to non-migrator in New Mexico

Food: seeds, plants, aquatic insects; will come to ground feeders offering corn

Compare: Female Gadwall (pg. 173) has a gray bill with orange sides. Female Northern Pintail (pg. 175) is similar to female Mallard, but it has a gray bill. Female Northern Shoveler (pg. 177) has a large spoon-shaped bill.

Stan's Notes: A familiar duck of lakes and ponds, it's considered a type of dabbling duck, tipping forward in shallow water to feed on aquatic plants on the bottom. The name "Mallard" comes from the Latin *masculus*, meaning "male," referring to the habit of males not taking part in raising ducklings. Both female and male have white tails and white underwings. Black central tail feathers of male curl upward. Will return to birthplace. Often associated with Mexican Mallard (see inset), which is the same size but has a yellow bill.

male pg. 269

female

GADWALL
Anas strepera

Size: 20" (50 cm)

Female: Very similar to the female Mallard. Mottled brown with pronounced color change from dark brown body to light brown neck and head. Wing linings are bright white, seen in flight. Small white wing patch, seen when swimming. Gray bill with orange sides.

Male: plump gray duck with a brown head and distinctive black rump, white belly, bright white wing linings, small white wing patch, chestnut-tinged wings, gray bill

Juvenile: similar to female

Nest: ground; female lines the nest with fine grass and down feathers plucked from her chest; 1 brood per year

Eggs: 8-11; white without markings

Incubation: 24-27 days; female incubates

Fledging: 48-56 days; young feed themselves

Migration: complete, to southwestern states, Mexico

Food: aquatic insects

Compare: The female Gadwall is very similar to female Mallard (pg. 171). Look for Gadwall's white wing patch and gray bill with orange sides.

Stan's Notes: A duck of shallow marshes. Consumes mostly plant material, dunking its head in water to feed rather than tipping forward, like other dabbling ducks. Walks well on land; feeds in fields and woodlands. Nests within 300 feet (100 m) of water. Often in pairs with other duck species. Establishes pair bond during winter.

173

male

female

NORTHERN PINTAIL
Anas acuta

YEAR-ROUND
WINTER

Size: 20" (50 cm), female
25" (63 cm), male

Male: A slender, elegant duck with a brown head, white neck, gray body and extremely long, narrow black tail. Gray bill. Non-breeding has a pale brown head that lacks the clear demarcation between the brown head and white neck. Lacks long tail feathers.

Female: mottled brown body with a paler head and neck, long tail, gray bill

Juvenile: similar to female

Nest: ground; female builds; 1 brood per year

Eggs: 6-9; olive green without markings

Incubation: 22-25 days; female incubates

Fledging: 36-50 days; female teaches young to feed

Migration: partial to complete, to southwestern states and Mexico

Food: aquatic plants and insects, seeds

Compare: The male Northern Pintail has a distinctive brown head and white neck. Look for the unique long tail feathers. The female Pintail is similar to female Mallard (pg. 171), but Mallard has an orange bill with black spots.

Stan's Notes: Common dabbling duck of marshes. Approximately 90 percent of its diet is aquatic plants from fresh water, except when females feed heavily on aquatic insects prior to nesting, presumably for extra nutrients for egg production. Male holds tail upright from water's surface. No other North American duck has such a long tail.

175

male pg. 289

female

NORTHERN SHOVELER
Anas clypeata

YEAR-ROUND
MIGRATION
WINTER

Size: 20" (50 cm)

Female: Medium-sized brown duck speckled with black. Blue wing patch. An extraordinarily large spoon-shaped bill, almost always held pointed toward the water.

Male: same spoon-shaped bill, iridescent green head, rusty sides and white breast

Juvenile: same as female

Nest: ground; female builds; 1 brood per year

Eggs: 9-12; olive without markings

Incubation: 22-25 days; female incubates

Fledging: 30-60 days; female leads young to food

Migration: complete migrator, to New Mexico, Mexico and Central America

Food: aquatic insects, plants

Compare: Similar color as female Mallard (pg. 171), but Mallard lacks the Shoveler's large bill. Female Redhead (pg. 167) is overall lighter brown and has a dark gray bill with a black tip. Look for Shoveler's large spoon-shaped bill to help identify.

Stan's Notes: One of several species of shoveler, so called because of the peculiar shape of its bill. The Northern Shoveler is the only species of these ducks in North America. Found in small flocks of 5-10, swimming low in water with its large bill pointed toward the water, as if it's too heavy to lift. Feeds mainly by filtering tiny aquatic insects and plants from the water's surface with its bill.

male pg. 267

female

BLUE GROUSE
Dendragapus obscurus

YEAR-ROUND

Size: 20" (50 cm)

Female: A mottled brown chicken-like bird with a gray belly. Yellow patch of skin above eyes (comb) is not as obvious as in males. Tail is darker brown and squared off.

Male: dark gray bird with bright yellow-to-orange patch of skin above eyes (comb)

Juvenile: similar to female

Nest: ground; female builds; 1 brood per year

Eggs: 6-12; pale white with brown markings

Incubation: 24-26 days; female incubates

Fledging: 7-10 days; female feeds young

Migration: non-migrator to partial migrator; will move around to find food

Food: insects, seeds, fruit, leaf buds and coniferous needles (Douglas-fir)

Compare: Smaller than female Ring-necked Pheasant (pg. 195) and lacking the long tail.

Stan's Notes: The most common grouse of the Rockies, seen from the foothills to the timberline. Usually on the ground, but also seen in trees feeding upon newly opened leaf buds in the spring. Often switches from an insect diet during summer to coniferous needles in winter. Male engages in elaborate courtship displays by fanning its tail, inflating its bright neck sac and singing (calling). Male mates with several females. Young leave nests within 24 hours and follow their mothers around to feed. Very tame and freezes if threatened, making it easy to get a close look.

male pg. 265

female

soaring

NORTHERN HARRIER
Circus cyaneus

YEAR-ROUND
WINTER

Size: 20" (50 cm); up to 3½-foot wingspan

Female: A slim, low-flying hawk. Dark brown back with brown-streaked breast and belly. Large white rump patch and narrow black bands across tail. Black wing tips. Yellow eyes.

Male: silver gray with large white rump patch and white belly, faint narrow bands across tail, black wing tips, yellow eyes

Juvenile: similar to female, with an orange breast

Nest: platform, often on ground; female and male build; 1 brood per year

Eggs: 4-8; bluish white without markings

Incubation: 31-32 days; female incubates

Fledging: 30-35 days; male and female feed young

Migration: partial to complete, to southwestern states, Mexico and Central America

Food: mice, snakes, insects, small birds

Compare: Slimmer than Red-tailed Hawk (pg. 183). Look for black bands on tail, a white rump patch and characteristic flight pattern to help identify.

Stan's Notes: One of the easiest hawks to identify. Harriers glide just above ground, following contours of the land while searching for prey. Holds its wings just above the horizontal position, tilting back and forth in the wind, similar to Turkey Vultures. Formerly called Marsh Hawk due to its habit of hunting over marshes. Feeds on the ground. Will perch on the ground to preen and rest. At any age, has a distinctive owl-like face disk.

soaring

Western

soaring

Eastern

RED-TAILED HAWK
Buteo jamaicensis

Size: 19-23" (48-58 cm); up to 4-foot wingspan

Male: A large hawk with a wide variety of colors from bird to bird, from chocolate brown to nearly all white. Usually a white breast and a distinctive brown belly band. Rust red tail, usually seen only from above. Underside of wing is white with a small dark patch on the leading edge near shoulder.

Female: same as male, only slightly larger

Juvenile: similar to adults, lacking the red tail, has a speckled chest and light eyes

Nest: platform; male and female build; 1 brood per year

Eggs: 2-3; white without markings or sometimes marked with brown

Incubation: 30-35 days; female and male incubate

Fledging: 45-46 days; male and female feed young

Migration: non-migrator to partial migrator

Food: mice, birds, snakes, insects, mammals

Compare: Swainson's Hawk (pg. 185) is slimmer with longer, more pointed wings and longer tail.

Stan's Notes: A common hawk of open country and in cities, often seen on freeway light posts, fences and in trees. Circles over open fields and roadsides, searching for prey. Large stick nest, lined with finer material such as evergreen tree needles. Nests are commonly seen in large trees along roads. Returns to same nest site every year. Develops red tail in the second year. Western variety has a brown chin; Eastern has a white chin. Map reflects the combined range.

soaring light morph

intermediate morph

light morph

dark morph

soaring dark morph

SWAINSON'S HAWK
Buteo swainsoni

SUMMER

Size: 21" (53 cm); up to 4½-foot wingspan

Male: Highly variable-plumaged hawk with three easily distinguishable color morphs. Light morph is brown with a white belly, a warm rusty breast and a white face. Intermediate has a dark breast, rusty belly and white at the base of the bill. Dark morph is nearly all dark brown with a rusty color low on belly.

Female: same as male

Juvenile: similar to adult

Nest: platform; female and male build; 1 brood per year

Eggs: 2-4; bluish or white, some brown markings

Incubation: 28-35 days; female and male incubate

Fledging: 28-30 days; female and male feed young

Migration: complete, to Central and South America

Food: small mammals, insects, snakes, birds

Compare: Slimmer than the Red-tailed (pg. 183) with longer, more pointed wings and longer tail. Rough-legged Hawk (pg. 187) has a lighter trailing edge of wings. Ferruginous Hawk (pg. 189) has a light trailing edge of wings.

Stan's Notes: A slender open country hawk that hunts mammals, insects, snakes and birds when soaring (kiting) or perching. Often flies with slightly upturned wings in a teetering, vulture-like flight. The light morph is the most common of the three color types, with intermediate and dark also common. Even minor nest disturbance can cause nest failure. Often gathers in large flocks to migrate.

185

dark morph

soaring dark morph

light morph

soaring light morph

ROUGH-LEGGED HAWK
Buteo lagopus

Size: 22" (56 cm); up to 4½-foot wingspan

Male: A hawk of several plumages. All plumages have a long tail with a dark band or bands. Distinctive dark wrists and belly. Relatively long wings, small bill and feet. Light morph has nearly pure white undersides of wings and base of tail. Dark morph is nearly all brown with light gray trailing edge of wings.

Female: same as male, only larger

Juvenile: same as adults

Nest: platform, on edge of cliff; female and male build; 1 brood per year

Eggs: 2-6; white without markings

Incubation: 28-31 days; female and male incubate

Fledging: 39-43 days; female and male feed young

Migration: complete, to the U.S.

Food: small animals, snakes, large insects

Compare: Similar size as Swainson's Hawk (pg. 185), which has narrow pointed wings, as seen in flight, and a lighter leading edge of wings unlike Rough-legged Hawk's lighter trailing edge of wings.

Stan's Notes: Two color morphs, light and dark, light being more common. Common winter resident, nesting in Canada's Northwest Territories and Alaska. More numerous in some years than others. It has much smaller and weaker feet than the other birds of prey, which means it must hunt smaller prey. Hunts from the air, usually hovering before diving for small rodents such as mice and voles.

soaring

soaring
juvenile

juvenile

FERRUGINOUS HAWK
Buteo regalis

Size: 23" (58 cm); up to 4½-foot wingspan

Male: Pale brown head, gray cheeks, reddish back and white chin, chest and belly. Rust flanks extend down feathered legs. Bright white undersides of wings, light rust wing linings. Tail white below, rust-tinged on top. Large, strong yellow feet. Red eyes. Dark eye line.

Female: same as male, but noticeably larger

Juvenile: brown head, nape, back and wings with a white chin, chest and belly

Nest: massive platform, low in a tree, sometimes on the ground; female and male construct; 1 brood per year

Eggs: 2-4; bluish or white, can have brown marks

Incubation: 28-33 days; female and male incubate

Fledging: 44-48 days; female and male feed young

Migration: non-migrator to partial in New Mexico

Food: larger mammals, snakes, insects, birds

Compare: Swainson's Hawk (pg. 185) is smaller and has a dark trailing edge of wings. Red-tailed Hawk (pg. 183) has a brown belly band and lacks rust flanks and legs.

Stan's Notes: The largest hawk species. Found in western prairies. Common name means "iron-like," referring to the rusty color. Male and female perform an aerial courtship, soaring with wings held above their backs, male diving at female, grabbing at each other with large, powerful feet. Often hunts larger mammals such as jack rabbits. Often stands on the ground. Nests in most of New Mexico.

GREATER ROADRUNNER
Geococcyx californianus

Size: 23" (58 cm)

Male: Overall brown with white streaking. Has a conspicuous crest that can be raised and lowered. An extremely long tail and a long, pointed brown bill. Blue patch just behind eyes. Short round wings are darker brown than body. Long gray legs with large feet.

Female: same as male

Juvenile: similar to adult

Nest: platform, low in a tree, shrub or cactus; the female and male build; 1-2 broods per year

Eggs: 4-6; white without markings

Incubation: 18-20 days; male and female incubate

Fledging: 16-18 days; male and female feed young

Migration: non-migrator

Food: insects, reptiles, small mammals and birds

Compare: This uniquely shaped ground dweller with an extremely long tail and prominent crest is hard to confuse with other birds.

Stan's Notes: Cuckoo family member known for running quickly across the ground to catch prey. A formidable predator, can run up to 15 miles (24 km) per hour. Flies short distances, usually in a low glide after a running takeoff. Raises its tail high, lowers it slowly. A slow, descending, low-pitched "coo-coo-coo-coo." Males do most incubating and feeding of the young. Performs a distraction display to protect nest. Young can catch prey four weeks after leaving nest.

YEAR-ROUND

GREAT HORNED OWL
Bubo virginianus

Size:	21-25" (53-63 cm); up to 3½-foot wingspan
Male:	Robust brown "horned" owl. Bright yellow eyes and V-shaped white throat resembling a necklace. Horizontal barring on the chest.
Female:	same as male, only slightly larger
Juvenile:	similar to adults, lacking ear tufts
Nest:	no nest; takes over the nests of crows, Great Blue Herons and hawks, or will use partial cavities, stumps or broken-off trees; 1 brood per year
Eggs:	2; white without markings
Incubation:	26-30 days; female incubates
Fledging:	30-35 days; male and female feed young
Migration:	non-migrator
Food:	mammals, birds (ducks), snakes, insects
Compare:	Burrowing Owl (pg. 145) is much smaller, has long legs and lacks the Great Horned's feather tuft "horns." Over twice the size of its cousin, Western Screech-Owl (pg. 237).

Stan's Notes: One of the earliest nesting birds in the state, laying eggs in January and February. Has excellent hearing; able to hear a mouse moving beneath a foot of snow. "Ears" are actually tufts of feathers (horns) and have nothing to do with hearing. Not able to turn its head all the way around. Wing feathers are ragged on ends, resulting in a silent flight. The eyelids close from the top down, like humans. Fearless, it is one of the few animals that will kill skunks and porcupines. Because of this, it is sometimes called Flying Tiger.

male

female

RING-NECKED PHEASANT
Phasianus colchicus

Size: 30-36" (76-90 cm), male, including tail
21-25" (53-63 cm), female, including tail

Male: Golden brown body with a long tail. White ring around neck with purple, green, blue and red head.

Female: smaller, less flamboyant all-brown bird with a long tail

Juvenile: similar to female, with a shorter tail

Nest: ground; female builds; 1 brood per year

Eggs: 8-10; olive brown without markings

Incubation: 23-25 days; female incubates

Fledging: 11-12 days; female leads young to food

Migration: non-migrator

Food: insects, seeds, fruit; visits ground feeders

Compare: The female Blue Grouse (pg. 179) is smaller than the female Ring-necked Pheasant and lacks the long tail. The male Ring-necked Pheasant is brightly colored.

Stan's Notes: Introduced from China in the late 1800s. Common now across the U.S. Like many other game birds, their numbers vary greatly, making them common in some years and scarce in others. "Ring-necked" refers to the thin white ring around the male's neck. "Pheasant" comes from the Greek word *phaisianos*, meaning "bird of the River Phasis." (The Phasis, located in Europe, is now known as the River Rioni.) Roosts on the ground or in trees at night. Listen for male's cackling call to attract females.

soaring

juvenile

GOLDEN EAGLE
Aquila chrysaetos

Size: 30-40" (76-102 cm); up to 7-foot wingspan

Male: Uniform dark brown with golden head and nape of neck. Yellow around the base of bill and yellow feet.

Female: same as male

Juvenile: similar to adult, but has white wrist patches and white base of tail

Nest: platform, on cliff; female and male build; 1 brood per year

Eggs: 2; white with brown markings

Incubation: 43-45 days; female and male incubate

Fledging: 66-75 days; female and male feed young

Migration: non-migrator to partial migrator; will move around to find food

Food: mammals, birds, reptiles, insects

Compare: Similar to Bald Eagle (pg. 59), lacking the white head and tail. Juvenile Golden Eagle, with its white wrist marks and base of tail, is often confused with juvenile Bald Eagle.

Stan's Notes: Large and powerful bird of prey that has no trouble taking larger prey such as jack rabbits. Hunts by perching or soaring and watching for movement. Inhabits mountainous terrain, requiring large territories to provide large supply of food. Thought to mate for life, renewing pair bond late in winter with spectacular high-flying courtship displays. Usually nests on cliff faces, rarely in trees. Uses well-established nest that has been used for generations. Not uncommon for it to add things to nest such as antlers, bones and barbed wire.

WILD TURKEY
Meleagris gallopavo

YEAR-ROUND

Size: 36-48" (90-120 cm)

Male: Large, plump brown and bronze bird with striking blue and red bare head. Fan tail and long, straight black beard in center of chest. Spurs on legs.

Female: thinner and less striking than male, usually lacking breast beard

Juvenile: same as adult of the same sex

Nest: ground; female builds; 1 brood per year

Eggs: 10-12; buff white with dull brown markings

Incubation: 27-28 days; female incubates

Fledging: 6-10 days; female leads young to food

Migration: non-migrator

Food: insects, seeds, fruit

Compare: This bird is quite distinctive and unlikely to be confused with others.

Stan's Notes: The largest native game bird in New Mexico, and the bird from which the domestic turkey was bred. Almost became our national bird, losing to the Bald Eagle by a single vote. A strong flier that can approach 60 miles (97 km) per hour. Able to fly straight up, then away. Eyesight is three times better than human eyesight. Hearing is also excellent; can hear competing males up to a mile away. Males hold "harems" of up to 20 females. Males are toms, females are hens and young are poults. Roosts in trees at night.

RUBY-CROWNED KINGLET
Regulus calendula

Size: 4" (10 cm)

Male: Small, teardrop-shaped green-to-gray bird with 2 white wing bars and a hidden ruby crown. White eye-ring.

Female: same as male, but lacking the ruby crown

Juvenile: same as female

Nest: pendulous; female builds; 1 brood per year

Eggs: 4-5; white with brown markings

Incubation: 11-12 days; female incubates

Fledging: 11-12 days; female and male feed young

Migration: complete, to southwestern states, Mexico, non-migrator in parts of New Mexico

Food: insects, berries

Compare: The female American Goldfinch (pg. 319) is larger, but shares the same olive color and unmarked breast. Look for the white eye-ring of Ruby-crowned Kinglet.

Stan's Notes: One of the smaller birds in the state. It takes a quick eye to see the male's ruby crown. Most commonly seen during the spring and fall migrations, when groups travel together. Look for it flitting around thick shrubs low to the ground. Female builds an unusual pendulous (sac-like) nest, intricately woven and decorated on the outside with colored lichens and mosses stuck together with spider webs. The nest is suspended from a branch overlapped by leaves and usually is hung high in a mature tree. The common name "Kinglet" comes from the Anglo-Saxon word *cyning*, or "king," referring to the male's ruby crown, and the diminutive suffix "let," meaning "small."

201

YEAR-ROUND

PYGMY NUTHATCH
Sitta pygmaea

Size: 4¼" (10.5 cm)

Male: Tiny gray-blue black bird with gray-brown crown. Creamy chest with a lighter chin. A relatively short tail, large head and long bill.

Female: same as male

Juvenile: same as adult

Nest: cavity; female and male construct; 1 brood per year

Eggs: 4-8; white with brown markings

Incubation: 14-16 days; female incubates

Fledging: 20-22 days; female and male feed young

Migration: non-migrator

Food: insects, berries, seeds; will visit seed feeders

Compare: Smaller than the Red-breasted Nuthatch (pg. 205) and the White-breasted Nuthatch (pg. 213). The Red-breasted has a rusty red chest unlike the creamy chest of the Pygmy Nuthatch. White-breasted Nuthatch has a distinctive black cap and a white chest.

Stan's Notes: A nuthatch of pine forests. Unlike the White-breasted Nuthatch, the Pygmy Nuthatch requires mature pines with old or decaying wood. Usually drills its own nest cavity. While it does not migrate, it forms winter flocks with chickadees and other birds and moves around to find food. Usually feeds in the crown of a tree or at the ends of twigs and branches, where it searches for insects and seeds. This is unlike White-breasted and Red-breasted Nuthatches, which usually search trunks of trees for food.

RED-BREASTED NUTHATCH
Sitta canadensis

YEAR-ROUND
WINTER

Size: 4½" (11 cm)

Male: A small gray-backed bird with a black cap and a prominent eye line. A rust red breast and belly.

Female: gray cap, pale undersides

Juvenile: same as female

Nest: cavity; female builds; 1 brood per year

Eggs: 5-6; white with red brown markings

Incubation: 11-12 days; female incubates

Fledging: 14-20 days; female and male feed young

Migration: non-migrator to irruptive migrator; moves around the state in search of food

Food: insects, seeds; visits seed and suet feeders

Compare: Slightly larger than the Pygmy Nuthatch (pg. 203) and smaller than White-breasted Nuthatch (pg. 213), neither of which has the rich red breast of the Red-breasted.

Stan's Notes: Red-breasted Nuthatch behaves like White-breasted and Pygmy Nuthatches, climbing down trunks of trees headfirst. Similar to chickadees, visits seed feeders, quickly grabbing a seed and flying off to crack it open. Will wedge a seed into a crevice and pound it open with several sharp blows. The name "Nuthatch" comes from the Middle English moniker *nuthak*, referring to the bird's habit of wedging a seed into a crevice and hacking it open. Look for it in mature conifers, frequently extracting seeds from cones. Doesn't excavate a cavity as the chickadee might; rather, it takes over a former woodpecker or chickadee cavity.

male

female

juvenile

VERDIN
Auriparus flaviceps

Size: 4½" (11 cm)

Male: Light gray to silvery overall. Lemon yellow head. Rusty red shoulder patch, frequently hidden. Short, pointed dark bill. Dark mark between bill and eyes. Dark legs and feet.

Female: duller than male

Juvenile: overall gray, lacks the yellow head, dark bill and rusty red shoulder patch

Nest: covered cup; male builds; 1-2 broods a year

Eggs: 4-5; bluish green with brown markings

Incubation: 8-10 days; female incubates

Fledging: 19-21 days; female and male feed young

Migration: non-migrator

Food: seeds, insects, fruit, nectar; comes to nectar feeders and orange halves

Compare: Smaller than Juniper Titmouse (pg. 217), which has a crest and lacks the yellow head. Mountain Chickadee (pg. 209) has an obvious black cap, chin and eye line.

Stan's Notes: A very friendly bird that can be a regular visitor to nectar feeders and orange halves. Often hides its rusty red shoulder marks, confusing the novice bird watcher. Most easily identified as a tiny gray bird with a yellow head. Male builds several ball-shaped, conspicuous nests of thorny twigs, interweaves them with leaves and grass and lines them with feathers and plant down. Male shows the nest possibilities to female and she selects one. After fledging, young return to nest at night unlike most small birds, which leave and don't return for shelter. Often uses nest for several seasons.

MOUNTAIN CHICKADEE
Poecile gambeli

YEAR-ROUND

Size: 5½" (14 cm)

Male: Overall gray with a black cap, chin and line through the eyes. White eyebrows.

Female: same as male

Juvenile: similar to adult

Nest: cavity, old woodpecker hole or excavates its own; female and male build; 1-2 broods per year

Eggs: 5-8; white without markings

Incubation: 11-14 days; female and male incubate

Fledging: 18-21 days; female and male feed young

Migration: non-migrator to partial migrator

Food: seeds, insects; visits seed and suet feeders

Compare: Slightly smaller than the Juniper Titmouse (pg. 217), which lacks a black cap and has a crest. Larger than Verdin (pg. 207), which has a yellow head.

Stan's Notes: An abundant bird in the state, but more common in coniferous forests in mountainous regions of New Mexico. Prefers old growth spruce, fir and pine forests. Feeds heavily on coniferous seeds and insects. Flocks with other birds during winter. Moves to lower elevations in winter, returning to high elevations for nesting. Excavates a nest cavity or uses an old woodpecker hole. Will use a nest box. Occasionally uses the same nest site year after year. Lines its nest with moss, hair and feathers. Female will not leave her nest if disturbed, but will hiss and flutter wings.

female
pg. 95

male

pink-sided

Oregon male

YEAR-ROUND
WINTER

DARK-EYED JUNCO
Junco hyemalis

Size: 5½" (14 cm)

Male: Round, dark-eyed bird with a slate gray-to-charcoal chest, head and back. White belly. Pink bill. Since the outermost tail feathers are white, tail appears as a white V in flight.

Female: same as male, only tan-to-brown color

Juvenile: similar to female, but has a streaked breast and head

Nest: cup; female and male construct; 2 broods per year

Eggs: 3-5; white with reddish brown markings

Incubation: 12-13 days; female incubates

Fledging: 10-13 days; male and female feed young

Migration: partial to non-migrator in New Mexico

Food: seeds, insects; will come to seed feeders

Compare: Rarely confused with any other bird. Small flocks feed under bird feeders in winter.

Stan's Notes: Several junco species have now been combined into one, simply called Dark-eyed Junco (see inset photos). A common year-round resident and one of the most numerous wintering birds in New Mexico. Females tend to migrate farther south than males. Spends the winter in foothills and plains after snowmelt; returns to higher elevations to nest. Nests in a wide variety of wooded habitats in April and May. Adhering to a rigid social hierarchy, dominant birds chase the less dominant birds. Look for its white outer tail feathers flashing in flight. Most comfortable on the ground, juncos "double-scratch" with both feet to expose seeds and insects. Eats many weed seeds. Usually is seen on the ground in small flocks.

211

WHITE-BREASTED NUTHATCH
Sitta carolinensis

YEAR-ROUND

Size: 5-6" (13-15 cm)

Male: Slate gray with a white face and belly, and black cap and nape. Long thin bill, slightly upturned. Chestnut undertail.

Female: similar to male, gray cap and nape

Juvenile: similar to female

Nest: cavity; female and male construct; 1 brood per year

Eggs: 5-7; white with brown markings

Incubation: 11-12 days; female incubates

Fledging: 13-14 days; female and male feed young

Migration: non-migrator

Food: insects, seeds; visits seed and suet feeders

Compare: Red-breasted Nuthatch (pg. 205) is smaller, with a rusty belly and distinctive black eye line. Pygmy Nuthatch (pg. 203) is smaller and lacks the White-breasted's black cap.

Stan's Notes: The nuthatch's habit of hopping headfirst down tree trunks helps it see insects and insect eggs that birds climbing up the trunk might miss. Incredible climbing agility comes from an extra-long hind toe claw or nail, nearly twice the size of the front toe claws. The name "Nuthatch" comes from the Middle English moniker *nuthak*, referring to the bird's habit of wedging a seed into a crevice and hacking it open. Frequently seen in mixed flocks of chickadees and Downy Woodpeckers. Mated pairs stay together all year, defending small territories. Listen for its characteristic spring call, "whi-whi-whi-whi," given from February through May. One of 17 worldwide nuthatch species.

female

Audubon's
male

Myrtle
male

female

first winter

YELLOW-RUMPED WARBLER
Dendroica coronata

YEAR-ROUND
MIGRATION
SUMMER
WINTER

Size: 5-6" (13-15 cm)

Male: Slate gray. Yellow patches on rump, flanks and head. Two white wing bars. Audubon's has a yellow chin. Myrtle has a white chin.

Female: duller than male, but same yellow patches

Juvenile: similar to female

Nest: cup; female builds; 2 broods per year

Eggs: 4-5; white with brown markings

Incubation: 12-13 days; female incubates

Fledging: 10-12 days; female and male feed young

Migration: non-migrator to partial migrator, southern New Mexico, Mexico and Central America

Food: insects, berries; rarely comes to suet feeders

Compare: Male Common Yellowthroat (pg. 321) has a yellow breast and very distinctive black mask. Male Yellow Warbler (pg. 325) is all yellow with orange streaks on the breast. Look for patches of yellow on the Yellow-rumped Warbler's rump, flanks and head to help identify.

Stan's Notes: A common warbler in the state. Nests in coniferous and aspen forests. Flocks of hundreds seen during migration in the fall when northern birds join resident populations for the winter, usually arriving in late September to early October. Male molts to a dull color in winter similar to female, retaining yellow patches. Sometimes called Butter-butts due to yellow patch on rump. Often called Audubon's Warbler in western states and Myrtle Warbler in eastern states. Familiar call is a robust "chip."

YEAR-ROUND

JUNIPER TITMOUSE
Baeolophus ridgwayi

Size: 6" (15 cm)

Male: An all-gray bird with a crest. Small gray bill. Dark eyes. May have a faint brown tinge to upper wings.

Female: same as male

Juvenile: similar to adult, often lighter in color, lacks a well-developed crest

Nest: cavity; female builds; 1 brood per year

Eggs: 3-6; white without markings

Incubation: 14-16 days; female and male incubate

Fledging: 16-21 days; female and male feed young

Migration: non-migrator

Food: seeds, insects, fruit

Compare: Slightly larger than Mountain Chickadee (pg. 209), which has a black cap and lacks a crest. Larger than the Verdin (pg. 207), which has a yellow head and lacks a crest.

Stan's Notes: A very drab-looking bird usually found in open dry habitats. Can be attracted to your yard with a nest box. The female does not usually fly when approached at the nest, but will fluff up and hiss to protect her eggs. Like the chickadee, it builds a similar nest with green moss and grass and lines it with animal fur. Mated pairs often remain together throughout the season. This species was once considered the same as the Oak Titmouse (*B. inornatus*).

male pg. 301

female

VERMILION FLYCATCHER
Pyrocephalus rubinus

Size: 6" (15 cm)

Female: A mostly gray bird with a gray head, neck and back. Nearly white chin and chest. Pink belly to undertail. Black tail. Thin black bill.

Male: crimson red head, crest, chin, breast and belly, black nape of neck, back, wings and tail, black line through eyes, thin black bill

Juvenile: similar to female, lacks a pink undertail

Nest: cup; female builds; 1-2 broods per year

Eggs: 2-4; white with brown markings

Incubation: 14-16 days; female and male incubate

Fledging: 14-16 days; female and male feed young

Migration: complete, to southern Arizona, throughout Mexico

Food: insects (mainly bees)

Compare: Similar body and bill shape as the phoebes of New Mexico and a similar habitat. Black Phoebe (pg. 37) is nearly all black with a white belly. The Say's Phoebe (pg. 223) has a pale orange belly.

Stan's Notes: A summer resident that is often in open areas with shrubs and small trees close to water. Will perch on a thin branch, pumping tail up and down while waiting for an aerial insect. Flies out to snatch it, then returns to the perch. Drops to the ground for terrestrial insects. Male raises its crest, fluffs chest feathers, fans tail and sings a song during a fluttery flight to court females. Female builds a shallow nest of twigs and grasses and lines it with downy plant material. Male feeds female during incubation and brooding.

WESTERN WOOD-PEWEE
Contopus sordidulus

Size: 6¼" (15.5 cm)

Male: An overall gray bird with darker wings and tail. Two narrow gray wing bars. Dull white throat with pale yellow or white belly. Black upper bill, dull orange lower.

Female: same as male

Juvenile: similar to adult, lacking the two-toned bill

Nest: cup; female builds; 1 brood per year

Eggs: 2-4; pale white with brown markings

Incubation: 12-14 days; female incubates

Fledging: 14-18 days; female and male feed young

Migration: complete, to Central and South America

Food: insects

Compare: Female Vermilion Flycatcher (pg. 219) is slightly smaller and has a pink lower belly. Black Phoebe (pg. 37) is larger and has a black head. Say's Phoebe (pg. 223) is larger and has a tawny belly.

Stan's Notes: A widespread bird in the state that is most common in aspen forests and near water. It requires trees with dead tops or branches from which to sing and hunt for flying insects, which compose nearly all of the diet. Often returns to the same perch after each foray. Nests throughout western North America from Alaska to Mexico. Overall populations are decreasing about 1 percent each year. Common name comes from a nasal whistle, "pee-wee."

SAY'S PHOEBE
Sayornis saya

Size: 7½" (19 cm)

Male: Overall dark gray, darkest on head, tail and wings. Belly and undertail tawny. Black bill.

Female: same as male

Juvenile: similar to adult, but browner overall with 2 tawny wing bars and a yellow lower bill

Nest: cup; female builds; 1-2 broods per year

Eggs: 3-6; pale white with brown markings

Incubation: 12-14 days; female incubates

Fledging: 14-16 days; female and male feed young

Migration: complete to partial, southern New Mexico, Mexico, Central and South America

Food: insects, berries

Compare: Western Wood-Pewee (pg. 221) is smaller and lacks a tawny belly. Female Vermilion Flycatcher (pg. 219) is smaller and has a pink belly.

Stan's Notes: A widespread bird in New Mexico below 9,000-foot (2,750 m) elevations. Nests in cliff crevices, abandoned buildings, bridges and other vertical structures. Frequently uses the same nest several times in a season, returning the following year to that same nest. A nearly all-insect diet. Flies out from perch to grab an aerial insect and returns to perch (hawking). Also hunts insects on the ground, hovering and dropping down to catch them. Classified as New World Flycatchers and not related to Old World Flycatchers. Named after Thomas Say, who is said to have discovered this bird in Colorado. The genus, species and first part of its common name refer to Mr. Say. "Phoebe" is likely an imitation of the bird's call.

AMERICAN DIPPER
Cinclus mexicanus

YEAR-ROUND

Size: 7½" (19 cm)

Male: Dark gray to black overall. Head is slightly lighter in color. A short upturned tail. Dark eyes and bill.

Female: same as male

Juvenile: similar to adult, only paler with white eyelids that are most noticeable when blinking

Nest: pendulous, covered nest with the entrance near the bottom, on cliff, behind waterfall; female builds; 1-2 broods per year

Eggs: 3-5; white without markings

Incubation: 13-17 days; female incubates

Fledging: 18-25 days; female and male feed young

Migration: non-migrator; seeks moving open water

Food: aquatic insects, small fish, crustaceans

Compare: Similar shape as American Robin (pg. 243), but lacks a red breast. The only songbird in the state that dives into fast-moving water.

Stan's Notes: A common bird of fast, usually noisy streams that provide some kind of protected shelf on which to construct a nest. Some have had success attracting with man-made ledges. Plunges headfirst into fast-moving water, looking for just about any aquatic insect, propelling itself underwater with its wings. Frequently seen emerging with a large insect, which it smashes against rock before eating. Has the ability to fly directly into the air from underwater. Depending on snowmelt, nesting usually starts in March or April. Dippers in lower elevations often nest a second time each season.

INCA DOVE
Columbina inca

Size: 8" (20 cm)

Male: A small thin-bodied dove, pale gray overall with a scalloped or scaly appearance due to dark-edged feathers. Lighter gray head with a dark thin bill and dark red eyes. Long thin tail. White outer tail feathers and dark rusty wing linings, seen in flight.

Female: same as male

Juvenile: similar to adult, lacks a scaly pattern

Nest: platform; female and male build; 2-3 broods per year

Eggs: 2; white without markings

Incubation: 12-14 days; female and male incubate

Fledging: 14-16 days; female and male feed young

Migration: non-migrator

Food: seeds, fruit; visits seed feeders on ground

Compare: One of the smallest doves in New Mexico. Scaly appearance assures its identification.

Stan's Notes: Seen in many habitats including cities and suburbs, mostly in arid areas with some low scrubby growth. Male bows to female with tail fanned to show white sides. Outer wing feathers produce a buzzing sound in flight. Groups of up to 50 birds gather in summer and winter to find food. Roosts in large groups, sitting side by side or sometimes one on another. Huddles in "pyramids," sometimes stacked 2-3 birds high. Constructs a loose platform nest of twigs, grass and leaves. Nest is sometimes built on the ground, low in a tree or shrub or in a hanging flower basket. Will also reuse the nest of a larger dove such as Mourning Dove.

female

male pg. 7

PHAINOPEPLA
Phainopepla nitens

Size: 8" (20 cm)

Female: Slim, long, mostly gray bird with a ragged crest and deep red eyes. Whitish wing bars.

Male: slim, long, glossy black bird with a ragged crest and deep red eyes, wing patches near tips of wings are white, obvious in flight

Juvenile: similar to female

Nest: cup; female and male construct; 1-2 broods per year

Eggs: 2-4; gray with brown markings

Incubation: 12-14 days; female and male incubate

Fledging: 18-20 days; female and male feed young

Migration: complete, to Arizona and California

Food: fruit (usually mistletoe), insects; will come to water elements or water drips in yards

Compare: Gray Jay (pg. 255) and Clark's Nutcracker (pg. 257) are similar, but both lack a crest.

Stan's Notes: Seen in desert scrub with water and mistletoe nearby. Gives a low, liquid "kweer" song, but will also mimic other species. In winter individuals defend food supply such as a single tree with abundant mistletoe berries. Probably responsible for the dispersal of mistletoe plants far and wide. Male will fly up to a height of 300 feet (90 m), circling and zigzagging to court female. Builds nest of twigs and plant fibers and binds it with spider webs in the crotch of a mistletoe cluster. Lines nest with hair or soft plant fibers. May be the only species to nest in two regions in the same nest season. Nests in dry desert habitat in early spring. When it gets hot, moves to a higher area with an abundant water supply to nest again.

EASTERN KINGBIRD
Tyrannus tyrannus

MIGRATION
SUMMER

Size: 8" (20 cm)

Male: Mostly black gray bird with white belly and chin. Black head and tail with a distinctive white band across the end of the tail. Has a concealed red crown that is rarely seen.

Female: same as male

Juvenile: same as adult

Nest: cup; male and female build; 1 brood a year

Eggs: 3-4; white with brown markings

Incubation: 16-18 days; female incubates

Fledging: 16-18 days; female and male feed young

Migration: complete, to Mexico, Central America and South America

Food: insects, fruit

Compare: Medium-sized bird, smaller than the Robin (pg. 243). Lacks any yellow of the Western Kingbird (pg. 337). Look for the white band at the end of Kingbird's tail to identify.

Stan's Notes: A summer resident and migrator seen in open fields and prairies. Autumn migration begins in late August and early September, with groups of up to 20 individuals migrating together. Returns to mating ground in spring, where male and female defend their territory. Acting unafraid of other birds and chasing the larger ones, it is perceived as having an attitude. Bold behavior gave rise to the common name, King. Perches on tall branches, watching for insects. After flying out to catch them, returns to the same perch, a technique called hawking. Becomes very vocal during late summer, when entire families call back and forth while hunting for insects.

TOWNSEND'S SOLITAIRE
Myadestes townsendi

YEAR-ROUND
WINTER

Size: 8½" (22 cm)

Male: All-gray robin look-alike with a prominent white ring around each eye. Wings slightly darker than the body. Long tail. Short dark bill and dark legs.

Female: same as male

Juvenile: darker gray with a tan scaly appearance

Nest: cup; female builds; 1-2 broods per year

Eggs: 3-5; blue, green, gray or white with brown markings

Incubation: 12-14 days; female incubates

Fledging: 10-14 days; female and male feed young

Migration: partial to complete, to southwestern states, Mexico; known to migrate to eastern states

Food: insects, fruit

Compare: American Robin (pg. 243) has a red breast. The Northern Mockingbird (pg. 245) lacks the white eye-ring. The Gray Jay (pg. 255) has a mostly white head. Clark's Nutcracker (pg. 257) has black wings.

Stan's Notes: A summer resident of coniferous mountain forests, moving lower in winter. "Hawks" for insects, perching in trees and darting out to capture them. Eats berries in winter when insects are not available and actively defends a good berry source from other birds. Builds nest on ground sheltered by rocks or an overhang, or sometimes low in a tree or shrub. Song is a series of clear flute-like whistles without a distinct pattern. Shows white outer tail feathers and light tan patches on wings when in flight.

233

SAGE THRASHER
Oreoscoptes montanus

MIGRATION
SUMMER
WINTER

Size: 8½" (22 cm)

Male: Light gray overall with a heavily streaked white breast. Distinctive white chin. Yellow orange eyes. Darker gray tail with white tip.

Female: same as male

Juvenile: duller version of adult

Nest: cup; female and male construct; 1-2 broods per year

Eggs: 3-5; blue with brown markings

Incubation: 13-17 days; female and male incubate

Fledging: 11-14 days; female and male feed young

Migration: complete, to southern New Mexico, Mexico and Central America

Food: insects, fruit

Compare: The Curve-billed Thrasher (pg. 251) lacks obvious streaks on the chest and has a long downward curving bill. The Cactus Wren (pg. 135) has bold white eyebrows and a down-curved bill. Mockingbird (pg. 245) has white wing patches, as seen in flight.

Stan's Notes: More common in the sagebrush regions of the state. Males are often seen and heard as they sing from the tops of shrubs. Constructs a large and bulky nest beneath or at the base of dense cover in an attempt to keep the nest shaded. Sometimes builds a twig platform over the nest if existing cover doesn't provide enough shade. Old nests are sometimes used by Gambel's Quails. Returns in April. Nests in May. Populations increasing in the state over the past few decades.

gray morph

brown morph

WESTERN SCREECH-OWL
Megascops kennicottii

YEAR-ROUND

Size: 8½" (22 cm); up to 1½-foot wingspan

Male: A small, overall gray owl with bright yellow eyes. Two short ear tufts. A short tail. Some birds are brownish.

Female: same as male

Juvenile: similar to adult of the same morph, lacks ear tufts

Nest: cavity; uses old woodpecker hole; 1 brood per year

Eggs: 2-6; white without markings

Incubation: 21-30 days; female incubates

Fledging: 25-30 days; female and male feed young

Migration: non-migrator

Food: insects, small mammals, birds

Compare: Burrowing Owl (pg. 145) is slightly larger and lacks ear tufts. Western Screech-Owl is hard to confuse with its considerably larger cousin, Great Horned Owl (pg. 193).

Stan's Notes: This is the most common small owl in New Mexico. An owl of suburban woodlands and backyards. Requires trees that are at least a foot in diameter for nesting and roosting, so it usually is found in towns or in trees that have been preserved. A secondary cavity nester, which means it nests in tree cavities created by other birds. Usually not found in elevations above 4,000 feet (1,200 m). Densities in lower areas are about 1 bird per square mile (2-3 birds per sq. km). Most screech-owls are gray; some are brown.

237

LOGGERHEAD SHRIKE
Lanius ludovicianus

Size: 9" (22.5 cm)

Male: A gray head and back with black wings and mask across the eyes. A white chin, breast and belly. Black tail, legs and feet. Black bill with hooked tip. White wing patches, seen in flight.

Female: same as male

Juvenile: dull version of adult

Nest: cup; male and female construct; 1-2 broods per year

Eggs: 4-7; off-white with dark markings

Incubation: 16-17 days; female incubates

Fledging: 17-21 days; female and male feed young

Migration: non-migrator in New Mexico

Food: insects, lizards, small mammals, frogs

Compare: The Northern Mockingbird (pg. 245) has a similar color pattern, but lacks the black mask. Shrike is stockier than Mockingbird and perches in more open places. Cedar Waxwing (pg. 125) has a black mask, but is brown, not gray and black like Shrike.

Stan's Notes: The Loggerhead is a songbird that acts like a bird of prey. Known for skewering prey on barbed wire fences, thorns and other sharp objects to store or hold still while tearing apart to eat, hence its other common name, Butcher Bird. Feet are too weak to hold the prey it eats. Breeding bird surveys indicate declining populations in the Great Plains due to pesticides killing its major food source–grasshoppers.

239

male

female

PYRRHULOXIA
Cardinalis sinuatus

YEAR-ROUND

Size: 9" (22.5 cm)

Male: Overall gray with a bright red-tipped crest, red mask, throat, breast, belly and edges of wings and tail. Stout yellow bill. Dark eyes.

Female: similar to male, lacking red on face, throat, breast and belly, bill is gray to dull yellow

Juvenile: similar to female, has a dark gray bill, lacks red highlights

Nest: cup; female builds; 1 brood per year

Eggs: 2-4; gray to green with brown markings

Incubation: 12-14 days; female and male incubate

Fledging: 8-10 days; female and male feed young

Migration: non-migrator

Food: seeds, fruit, insects; will visit water elements and ground feeders

Compare: Unique-looking bird that is rarely confused with any other. Look for the tall crest and thick bill to help identify.

Stan's Notes: This is a secretive bird of arid brush, thorn scrub and mesquite habitat. Like its cousin, the Northern Cardinal, it is most active in early morning and just before sunset. Has a similar loud, crisp song like the cardinal and a single metallic "chip" call. Small flocks move around in the winter to find food. Feeds mostly on the ground, eating grass seeds and insects. Male feeds female during courtship and incubation. Female constructs a nest with twigs and grass in dense shrubs or thickets and lines it with fine grasses and plant fibers. Both defend home territory during the breeding season. Use water elements and ground feeders to attract it to your yard.

male

female

AMERICAN ROBIN
Turdus migratorius

Size: 9-11" (22.5-28 cm)

Male: A familiar gray bird with a rusty red breast, and nearly black head and tail. White chin with black streaks. White eye-ring.

Female: similar to male, but with a gray head and a duller breast

Juvenile: similar to female, but has a speckled breast and brown back

Nest: cup; female builds with help from the male; 2-3 broods per year

Eggs: 4-7; pale blue without markings

Incubation: 12-14 days; female incubates

Fledging: 14-16 days; female and male feed young

Migration: complete migrator, to southwestern states, Mexico and Central America, non-migrator in New Mexico

Food: insects, fruit, berries, worms

Compare: Familiar bird to all.

Stan's Notes: Although a complete migrator in northern states, it is a year-round resident in New Mexico. Can be heard singing all night long during springtime. Most people don't realize how easy it is to differentiate the male and female robins. Compare the male's dark, nearly black head and brick red breast with the female's gray head and dull red breast. Robins are not listening for worms when they cock their heads to one side. They are looking with eyes that are placed far back on the sides of their heads. A very territorial bird. Often seen fighting its own reflection in windows.

displaying

NORTHERN MOCKINGBIRD
Mimus polyglottos

YEAR-ROUND

Size: 10" (25 cm)

Male: Silvery gray head and back with light gray chest and belly. White wing patches, seen in flight or during display. Tail mostly black with white outer tail feathers. Black bill.

Female: same as male

Juvenile: dull gray, a heavily streaked chest, gray bill

Nest: cup; female and male build; 2 broods per year, sometimes more

Eggs: 3-5; blue green with brown markings

Incubation: 12-13 days; female incubates

Fledging: 11-13 days; female and male feed young

Migration: non-migrator in New Mexico

Food: insects, fruit

Compare: Loggerhead Shrike (pg. 239) has a similar color pattern, but is stockier, has a black mask and perches in more open places. Townsend's Solitaire (pg. 233) has a white eye-ring. Look for Mockingbird to spread its wings, flash its white wing patches and wag its tail from side to side.

Stan's Notes: Very animated. Performs an elaborate mating dance. Facing each other with heads and tails erect, pairs run toward each other, flashing white wing patches, and then retreat to cover nearby. Thought to flash wing patches to scare up insects when hunting. Sits for long periods of time on top of a shrub. Imitates other birds (vocal mimicry), hence the common name. Young males often sing at night. Often unafraid of people, allowing for close observation.

male

female

GAMBEL'S QUAIL
Callipepla gambelii

Size: 10" (25 cm)

Male: A plump round bird with a short tail. Gray chest, back and tail. Rusty crest outlined in white. Dark chin, throat and forehead with a unique dark plume emanating from the forehead. Rusty sides with white streaks. A dark patch on belly. Black bill. Gray legs.

Female: similar to male, lacks a rusty crest and dark chin, throat and forehead, plume less robust

Juvenile: similar to female

Nest: ground; female builds; 1-2 broods per year

Eggs: 8-12; dull white with brown markings

Incubation: 21-24 days; female incubates

Fledging: 7-10 days; female and male show the young what to eat

Migration: non-migrator

Food: seeds, leaves, insects, fruit; comes to seed feeders on the ground

Compare: Same size as Scaled Quail (pg. 249). Look for Gambel's unique plume to help identify.

Stan's Notes: A native species. Prefers arid scrubby regions with a constant water source. Winter flocks of up to 20 birds (coveys) split up during breeding season. Covey walks in single file. Able to hop on and over fences. Scurries across open areas to reach cover. Visits feeders in early morning and late afternoon. Takes dust baths in dirt depressions, kicking dust over body to get rid of small insects. Builds cup nest under vegetation, lining it with grass and feathers. Male gives a distinctive, repetitious call, "yup-waay-yup-yup."

SCALED QUAIL
Callipepla squamata

Size: 10" (25 cm)

Male: Overall gray with a prominent white-tipped crest. Scaly appearance due to black-tipped feathers on gray neck, chest and belly. Short gray tail. Small black bill. Dark eyes. Gray legs and feet.

Female: same as male

Juvenile: similar to adult

Nest: ground; female builds; 1 brood per year

Eggs: 12-14; white with or without markings

Incubation: 21-23 days; female incubates

Fledging: 3-7 days; female and male show the young what to eat

Migration: non-migrator

Food: seeds, leaves, insects, fruit; comes to seed feeders on the ground

Compare: Gambel's Quail (pg. 247) has a plume on forehead and longer tail. Scaled Quail lacks the male Gambel's black throat patch. Look for the white-tipped crest to help identify.

Stan's Notes: Similar activities and behaviors as Gambel's Quail. Hybridizes with Gambel's Quails where large populations overlap. Forms large winter flocks of up to 100 birds called coveys. Smaller groups in summer. Dominant males perch on elevated perches to watch for predators. Unmated males call from perches, looking for females. During courtship male raises crest and droops wings for female. Female scrapes a depression in the ground in tall grass or under shrubs and lines nest with dried grass and a few feathers.

CURVE-BILLED THRASHER
Toxostoma curvirostre

YEAR-ROUND

Size: 11" (28 cm)

Male: Large-bodied bird with a long tail and long downward-curved bill. Overall gray to light brown with faint spots on breast and belly. Eyes are dark yellow to orange.

Female: same as male

Juvenile: similar to adult, with a shorter bill

Nest: cup; female and male construct; 1-2 broods per year

Eggs: 3-4; pale blue green with brown markings

Incubation: 12-14 days; female and male incubate

Fledging: 14-18 days; female and male feed young

Migration: non-migrator

Food: insects, fruit, seeds; comes to seed feeders on the ground and water elements

Compare: The Sage Thrasher (pg. 235) has obvious streaks on the chest. Larger than the Cactus Wren (pg. 135), which has a spotty dark patch on chest and chestnut brown crown.

Stan's Notes: A familiar backyard bird that prefers scrubby desert habitat with mesquite, cactus and cholla. Will drive out any Cactus Wrens in its territory. Calls a loud, two-syllable "whit-wee." Feeds on the ground. Male follows female during courtship, singing a soft song. Builds nest in a spiny shrub or cactus, using twigs and grass and lining it with finer plant material. Will often reuse the nest after making minor repairs. Pairs often remain together all year. Young hatch on sequential days, requiring the parents to brood young for over two weeks. In hot weather parents shade the young from sun.

WHITE-WINGED DOVE
Zenaida asiatica

YEAR-ROUND
SUMMER

Size: 11" (28 cm)

Male: A light gray to brown with a conspicuous white edge on the wings. Small black dash under cheeks. Surrounding bright red eyes are vivid blue eye-rings. In flight, a white patch across the middle of the wings with black wing tips.

Female: same as male

Juvenile: similar to adult

Nest: platform; female and male build; 2-3 broods per year

Eggs: 2-4; white without markings

Incubation: 13-14 days; female and male incubate

Fledging: 13-16 days; female and male feed young

Migration: partial migrator to non-migrator

Food: seeds, fruit; will come to seed feeders

Compare: Slightly smaller than the Mourning Dove (pg. 155), which lacks the white line on closed wings, and white and black pattern of the White-winged Dove in flight.

Stan's Notes: Very similar to the Mourning Dove in behavior and appearance. Feeds on the ground, pecking at seeds and tiny grains of rock to aid digestion. Parents feed young a regurgitated liquid called crop-milk the first few days of life. Male uses its white and black wing coloration to display to mate. May nest alone or in large colonies. This non-native species was introduced during the 1950s when captive birds were released in Florida. Gives a distinctive call, "coo-cuk-ca-roo."

GRAY JAY
Perisoreus canadensis

Size: 11½" (29 cm)

Male: Large gray bird with a white forehead and nape of neck. Short black bill. Dark eyes.

Female: same as male

Juvenile: sooty gray with a faint white whisker mark

Nest: cup; male and female construct; 1 brood per year

Eggs: 3-4; gray white, finely marked to unmarked

Incubation: 16-18 days; female incubates

Fledging: 14-15 days; male and female feed young

Migration: non-migrator

Food: insects, seeds, fruit, nuts; visits seed feeder

Compare: Slightly larger than the Western Scrub-Jay (pg. 77), Pinyon Jay (pg. 79) and Steller's Jay (pg. 81), but lacks blue coloring. Clark's Nutcracker (pg. 257) is slightly larger with black wings. Female Phainopepla (pg. 229) has a crest and lacks the Gray Jay's white forehead and nape.

Stan's Notes: A bird of coniferous woods in mid to high elevations. Called Camp Robber because it rummages through camps looking for scraps of food. Also known as Whisky Jack or Canada Jay. Easily tamed, it will fly to your hand if offered raisins or nuts. Will eat just about anything. Also stores extra food for winter, balling it together in a sticky mass, placing it on a tree limb, often concealing it with lichen or bark. Travels around in family units of 3-5, making good companions for campers, canoeists and high altitude hikers and climbers. Reminds some of an overgrown chickadee.

CLARK'S NUTCRACKER
Nucifraga columbiana

YEAR-ROUND

Size: 12" (30 cm)

Male: Gray with black wings and a narrow black band down the center of tail. Small white patches on long wings, seen in flight. Has a relatively short tail with a white undertail.

Female: same as male

Juvenile: same as adult

Nest: cup; female and male build; 1 brood a year

Eggs: 2-5; pale green with brown markings

Incubation: 16-18 days; female and male incubate

Fledging: 18-20 days; female and male feed young

Migration: non-migrator

Food: seeds, insects, berries, eggs, mammals

Compare: Slightly larger than the Gray Jay (pg. 255), which lacks the Nutcracker's black wings. Townsend's Solitaire (pg. 233) is smaller, lacks black wings and has a smaller bill. The Steller's Jay (pg. 81) is dark blue with a black crest. Female Phainopepla (pg. 229) has a crest and lacks a white undertail.

Stan's Notes: A high country bird found in coniferous forests in New Mexico. It has a varied diet, but relies heavily on piñon seeds, often caching large quantities to consume later or feed to young. Has a large pouch in its throat (sublingual pouch), which it uses to transport seeds. Studies show the birds can carry up to 100 seeds at a time. Nests early in the year, often while snow still covers the ground, relying on stored foods. A "Lewis and Clark" bird, first recorded by William Clark in 1805 in Idaho.

soaring

juvenile

SHARP-SHINNED HAWK
Accipiter striatus

YEAR-ROUND
WINTER

Size: 10-14" (25-36 cm); up to 2-foot wingspan

Male: Small woodland hawk with a gray back and head and a rusty red breast. Long tail with several dark tail bands, widest band at end of squared-off tail. Red eyes.

Female: same as male, only larger

Juvenile: same size as adults, with a brown back and heavily streaked breast, yellow eyes

Nest: platform; female builds; 1 brood per year

Eggs: 4-5; white with brown markings

Incubation: 32-35 days; female incubates

Fledging: 24-27 days; female and male feed young

Migration: complete migrator, to southwestern states, Mexico and Central America, non-migrator in half of New Mexico

Food: birds, small mammals

Compare: Similar to Cooper's Hawk (pg. 263), only smaller. Cooper's has a larger head, slightly longer neck and rounded tail. Look for Sharp-shinned's squared tail to help identify.

Stan's Notes: A common hawk of backyards and woodlands, often seen swooping in on birds visiting feeders. Its short rounded wings and long tail allow this hawk to navigate through thick stands of trees in pursuit of prey. Common name comes from the sharp keel on the leading edge of its "shin," though it is actually below rather than above the bird's ankle on the tarsus bone of foot. The tarsus in most birds is round. In flight, head doesn't protrude as far as the head of the Cooper's Hawk.

259

ROCK PIGEON
Columba livia

YEAR-ROUND

Size: 13" (33 cm)

Male: No set color pattern. Gray to white, patches of iridescent greens and blues, usually with a light rump patch.

Female: same as male

Juvenile: same as adult

Nest: platform; female builds; 3-4 broods per year

Eggs: 1-2; white without markings

Incubation: 18-20 days; female and male incubate

Fledging: 25-26 days; female and male feed young

Migration: non-migrator

Food: seeds

Compare: Mourning Dove (pg. 155) is smaller, light brown and lacks all the color variations of the Rock Pigeon.

Stan's Notes: Also known as Domestic Pigeon, formerly known as Rock Dove. Introduced to North America from Europe by the early settlers. This bird is most common around cities and barnyards, where it scratches for seeds. One of the few birds that has a wide variety of colors, produced by years of selective breeding while in captivity. Parents feed their young a regurgitated liquid known as crop-milk for the first few days of life. One of the few birds that can drink without tilting its head back. Nests under bridges and on buildings, balconies, barns and sheds. Was once poisoned as a "nuisance city bird." Many cities now have Peregrine Falcons (not shown) that feed on Rock Pigeons, keeping their numbers in check.

soaring

juvenile

COOPER'S HAWK
Accipiter cooperii

Size: 14-20" (36-50 cm); up to 2½-foot wingspan

Male: Medium-sized hawk with short wings and long rounded tail with several black bands. Rusty breast and dark wing tips. Slate gray back. Bright yellow spot at base of gray bill (cere). Dark red eyes.

Female: similar to male, only slightly larger

Juvenile: brown back with brown streaks on breast, bright yellow eyes

Nest: platform; male and female build; 1 brood per year

Eggs: 2-4; greenish with brown markings

Incubation: 32-36 days; female and male incubate

Fledging: 28-32 days; male and female feed young

Migration: non-migrator to partial migrator; will move around to find food

Food: small birds, mammals

Compare: Nearly identical to the Sharp-shinned Hawk (pg. 259), only larger, darker gray and with a rounded-off tail.

Stan's Notes: Resident hawk in New Mexico. In flight, look for its large head, short wings and long tail. The short stubby wings help it maneuver between trees while pursuing small birds. Comes to feeders, hunting for unaware birds. Flies with long glides followed by a few quick flaps. Known to ambush prey, it will fly into heavy brush or even run on the ground in pursuit. Nestlings have gray eyes that become bright yellow at 1 year of age and dark red later.

female pg. 181

male

soaring

NORTHERN HARRIER
Circus cyaneus

Size: 20" (50 cm); up to 3½-foot wingspan

Male: A slim, low-flying hawk. Silver gray with a large white rump patch and a white belly. Faint narrow bands across tail. Black wing tips. Yellow eyes.

Female: dark brown back, a brown-streaked breast and belly, large white rump patch, narrow black bands across the tail, black wing tips, yellow eyes

Juvenile: similar to female, with an orange breast

Nest: platform, often on ground; female and male build; 1 brood per year

Eggs: 4-8; bluish white without markings

Incubation: 31-32 days; female incubates

Fledging: 30-35 days; male and female feed young

Migration: partial to complete, to southwestern states, Mexico and Central America

Food: mice, snakes, insects, small birds

Compare: Slimmer than Red-tailed Hawk (pg. 183). Look for black tail bands, white rump patch and characteristic flight to help identify.

Stan's Notes: One of the easiest hawks to identify. Harriers glide just above ground, following contours of the land while searching for prey. Holds its wings just above the horizontal position, tilting back and forth in the wind, similar to Turkey Vultures. Formerly called Marsh Hawk due to its habit of hunting over marshes. Feeds on the ground. Will perch on the ground to preen and rest. At any age, has a distinctive owl-like face disk.

female pg. 179

male

BLUE GROUSE
Dendragapus obscurus

YEAR-ROUND

Size: 20" (50 cm)

Male: Dark gray chicken-like bird. Bright yellow-to-orange patch of skin above eyes (comb). While displaying, white feathers surround an inflated yellow or purplish sac. Fans a gray-tipped, nearly black tail.

Female: mottled brown, gray belly, yellow patch of skin above eyes (comb)

Juvenile: similar to female

Nest: ground; female builds; 1 brood per year

Eggs: 6-12; pale white with brown markings

Incubation: 24-26 days; female incubates

Fledging: 7-10 days; female feeds young

Migration: non-migrator to partial migrator; will move around to find food

Food: insects, seeds, fruit, leaf buds and coniferous needles (Douglas-fir)

Compare: Gambel's Quail (pg. 247) is half the size of Blue Grouse and has a plume on forehead.

Stan's Notes: The most common grouse of the Rockies, seen from the foothills to the timberline. Usually on the ground, but also seen in trees feeding upon newly opened leaf buds in the spring. Often switches from an insect diet during summer to coniferous needles in winter. Male engages in elaborate courtship displays by fanning its tail, inflating its bright neck sac and singing (calling). Male mates with several females. Young leave nests within 24 hours and follow their mothers around to feed. Very tame and freezes if threatened, making it easy to get a close look.

female pg. 173

male

GADWALL
Anas strepera

**YEAR-ROUND
WINTER**

Size: 20" (50 cm)

Male: A plump gray duck with a brown head and a distinctive black rump. White belly and chestnut-tinged wings. Bright white wing linings. Small white wing patch, seen when swimming. Gray bill.

Female: similar to female Mallard, a mottled brown with a pronounced color change from dark brown body to light brown neck and head, bright white wing linings, small white wing patch, gray bill with orange sides

Juvenile: similar to female

Nest: ground; female lines the nest with fine grass and down feathers plucked from her chest; 1 brood per year

Eggs: 8-11; white without markings

Incubation: 24-27 days; female incubates

Fledging: 48-56 days; young feed themselves

Migration: complete, to southwestern states, Mexico

Food: aquatic insects

Compare: Male Gadwall is one of the few gray ducks. Look for its distinctive black rump.

Stan's Notes: A duck of shallow marshes. Consumes mostly plant material, dunking its head in water to feed rather than tipping forward, like other dabbling ducks. Walks well on land; feeds in fields and woodlands. Nests within 300 feet (100 m) of water. Often in pairs with other duck species. Establishes pair bond during winter. Mostly commonly seen in winter.

in flight

CANADA GOOSE
Branta canadensis

YEAR-ROUND
WINTER

Size: 25-43" (63-109 cm); up to 5½-foot wingspan

Male: Large gray goose with a black neck and head and a white chin or cheek strap.

Female: same as male

Juvenile: same as adult

Nest: platform, on the ground; female builds; 1 brood per year

Eggs: 5-10; white without markings

Incubation: 25-30 days; female incubates

Fledging: 42-55 days; male and female teach young to feed

Migration: partial to complete, to southwestern states, non-migrator in parts of New Mexico

Food: aquatic plants, insects, seeds

Compare: Large goose that is rarely confused with any other bird.

Stan's Notes: Common winter residents throughout New Mexico. Adults mate for many years, but only start to breed in their third year. Males often act as sentinels, standing at the edge of a group, bobbing their heads up and down, becoming very aggressive to anybody who approaches. Will hiss as if displaying displeasure. Adults molt primary flight feathers while raising young, rendering family groups flightless at the same time. Several subspecies vary geographically around the U.S. Generally they are darker in color in western groups and paler in eastern. Size decreases northward, with the smallest subspecies found on the Arctic tundra.

in flight

rusty stain

rusty stain
in flight

SANDHILL CRANE
Grus canadensis

MIGRATION
WINTER

Size: 40-48" (102-120 cm); up to 7-foot wingspan

Male: Elegant gray bird with long legs and neck. Wings and body often stained rusty brown. Scarlet red cap. Yellow-to-red eyes.

Female: same as male

Juvenile: dull brown, lacks red cap, has yellow eyes

Nest: platform, on the ground; female and male build; 1 brood per year

Eggs: 2; olive with brown markings

Incubation: 28-32 days; female and male incubate

Fledging: 65 days; female and male feed young

Migration: complete, to southern New Mexico, Mexico

Food: insects, fruit, worms, plants, amphibians

Compare: Similar size as Great Blue Heron (pg. 275), but Sandhill has a shorter bill and red cap. Great Blue Heron flies with neck held in an S shape unlike the Sandhill's straight neck.

Stan's Notes: Among the tallest birds in the world and capable of flying at great heights. Usually seen in large undisturbed fields near water. Has a very distinctive rattling call. Often heard before seen. Plumage often appears rusty brown (see insets) due to staining from mud during preening. A characteristic flight with upstroke quicker than down. Performing a spectacular mating dance, the birds face each other, bow and jump into the air while uttering loud cackling sounds and flapping wings. Often flips sticks and grass into the air during dance. Thousands of cranes overwinter in the southern half of New Mexico. Many people travel great distances just to see this natural spectacle.

in flight

GREAT BLUE HERON
Ardea herodias

YEAR-ROUND
MIGRATION

Size: 42-52" (107-132 cm); up to 6-foot wingspan

Male: Tall gray heron. Black eyebrows extend into several long plumes off the back of head. Long yellow bill. Feathers at base of neck drop down in a kind of necklace.

Female: same as male

Juvenile: same as adult, but more brown than gray, with a black crown and no plumes

Nest: platform; male and female build; 1 brood per year

Eggs: 3-5; blue green without markings

Incubation: 27-28 days; female and male incubate

Fledging: 56-60 days; male and female feed young

Migration: complete migrator, to southwestern states, Mexico, Central America, South America, non-migrator in most of New Mexico

Food: small fish, frogs, insects, snakes

Compare: Similar size as the Sandhill Crane (pg. 273), but lacks the Sandhill's red crown. Sandhill Crane flies with neck held straight unlike the Great Blue Heron's S-shaped neck.

Stan's Notes: One of the most common herons, often barking like a dog when startled. Seen stalking small fish in shallow water. Will strike at mice, squirrels and just about anything else it might come across. Flies holding neck in an S shape, with its long legs trailing straight out behind. The wings are held in cupped fashion during flight. Nests in colonies of up to 100 birds. Nests in treetops near or over open water.

male

female

SUMMER

BLACK-CHINNED HUMMINGBIRD
Archilochus alexandri

Size: 3¾" (9.5 cm)

Male: Tiny iridescent green bird with black throat patch (gorget) that reflects violet blue in sunlight. Black chin. White chest and belly.

Female: same as male, but lacking the throat patch and black chin, has white flanks

Juvenile: similar to female

Nest: cup; female builds; 1-2 broods per year

Eggs: 1-3; white without markings

Incubation: 13-16 days; female incubates

Fledging: 19-21 days; female feeds young

Migration: complete, to Central and South America

Food: nectar, insects; will come to nectar feeders

Compare: Slightly smaller than the male Broad-tailed Hummingbird (pg. 279), which has a rosy red throat patch and lacks a black chin. The flanks of female Broad-tailed (pg. 279) are tan, not white, like female Black-chinned's.

Stan's Notes: One of the smallest birds in New Mexico and one of several hummingbird species in the state. Able to fly backward, but it doesn't sing. Will chatter or buzz to communicate. Wings create a humming noise, flapping nearly 80 times per second. Weighing 2-3 gm, it takes about five average-sized hummingbirds to equal the weight of one chickadee. Males return first at the end of April. Male performs a spectacular pendulum-like flight over a perched female. After mating, the female builds a nest, using spider webs to glue nest materials together, and raises young without mate's help. More than one clutch per year not uncommon.

male

female

BROAD-TAILED HUMMINGBIRD
Selasphorus platycercus

Size: 4" (10 cm)

Male: Tiny iridescent green bird with black throat patch (gorget) that reflects rosy red in sunlight. Wings and part of the back are green. White chest.

Female: same as male, but lacking the throat patch, much more green on back, tan flanks

Juvenile: similar to female

Nest: cup; female builds; 1-2 broods per year

Eggs: 1-3; white without markings

Incubation: 12-14 days; female incubates

Fledging: 20-22 days; female feeds young

Migration: complete, to Central and South America

Food: nectar, insects; will come to nectar feeders

Compare: Slightly larger than the male Black-chinned Hummingbird (pg. 277), which has violet blue throat patch and a black chin. Female Black-chinned (pg. 277) has white flanks unlike the tan flanks of female Broad-tailed.

Stan's Notes: Hummingbirds are the only birds with the ability to fly backward. Does not sing. Will chatter or buzz to communicate. Wing beats produce a whistle, almost like a tiny ringing bell. Heart pumps an incredible 1,260 beats per minute. Weighing 2-3 gm, it takes about five average-sized hummingbirds to equal the weight of a single chickadee. Male performs a spectacular pendulum-like flight over the perched female. After mating, female builds nest and raises young without any help from her mate. Constructs a soft, flexible nest that expands to accommodate the growing young.

male

female

VIOLET-GREEN SWALLOW
Tachycineta thalassina

MIGRATION
SUMMER

Size: 5¼" (13.5 cm)

Male: Dull emerald green crown, nape and back. Violet blue wings and tail. White chest and belly. White cheeks with white extending above the eyes. Wings extend beyond the tail when perching.

Female: same as male, only duller

Juvenile: similar to adult of the same sex

Nest: cavity; female and male construct; 1 brood per year

Eggs: 4-6; pale white with brown markings

Incubation: 13-14 days; female incubates

Fledging: 18-24 days; female and male feed young

Migration: complete, to Central and South America

Food: insects

Compare: Similar size as the Cliff Swallow (pg. 101), which has a distinctive tan-to-rust pattern on the head. Barn Swallow (pg. 69) has a distinctive, deeply forked tail. Tree Swallow (pg. 67) is mostly a deep blue, lacking any emerald green of the Violet-green Swallow.

Stan's Notes: A solitary nester in tree cavities, but rarely beneath cliff overhangs unlike the colony-nesting Cliff Swallow. Like Tree Swallows, can be attracted with a nest box. Will search for miles for errant feathers to line its nest. A short tail with wing tips extending beyond the end of the tail when perching. Returns to New Mexico in April. Begins nesting right away. Young often leave nest by June.

GREEN-TAILED TOWHEE
Pipilo chlorurus

Size: 7¼" (18.5 cm)

Male: A unique yellowish green back, wings and tail. Dark gray chest and face. Bright white throat with black stripes. Rusty red crown.

Female: same as male

Juvenile: olive green with heavy streaking on breast and belly, lacks crown and throat markings of adult

Nest: cup; female and male construct; 1-2 broods per year

Eggs: 3-5; white with brown markings

Incubation: 12-14 days; female and male incubate

Fledging: 10-14 days; female and male feed young

Migration: complete, to southern New Mexico, Mexico and Central America

Food: insects, seeds, fruit

Compare: Canyon Towhee (pg. 141) has a distinctive necklace of dark spots. The Spotted Towhee (pg. 9) is black with rusty sides. The Green-tailed's unusual color, short wings, long tail and large bill make it easy to identify.

Stan's Notes: A common bird of shrubby hillsides and sagebrush mountain slopes as high as 7,000 feet (2,150 m). Like other towhee species, searches for insects and seeds, taking a little jump forward while kicking backward with both feet. Known for scurrying away from trouble by jumping to ground without opening its wings and then running across the ground. Arrives in northern New Mexico in April. Begins breeding in May.

LEWIS'S WOODPECKER
Melanerpes lewis

Size: 10¾" (27.5 cm)

Male: Dull green head and back. Distinctive gray collar and breast. Deep red face and a light red belly.

Female: same as male

Juvenile: similar to adult, with a brown head, lacking the red face

Nest: cavity; male and female excavate; 1 brood per year

Eggs: 4-8; white without markings

Incubation: 13-14 days; female and male incubate

Fledging: 28-34 days; female and male feed young

Migration: non-migrator to partial migrator; will move around to find food in winter

Food: insects, nuts, seeds, berries

Compare: Red-naped Sapsucker (pg. 41) has a black-and-white pattern on back and much more red on the head.

Stan's Notes: Large and handsome woodpecker of western states. First collected and named in 1805 by Lewis and Clark in Montana. During breeding season, it feeds exclusively on insects rather than grubs, like other woodpeckers. Prefers open pine forests and areas with recent forest fires. Excavates in dead or soft wood. Uses same cavity year after year. Tends to mate for long term. Moves around in winter to search for food such as pine nuts (seeds).

female pg. 171

male

Mexican

MALLARD
Anas platyrhynchos

**YEAR-ROUND
WINTER**

Size: 19-21" (48-53 cm)

Male: Large, bulbous green head, white necklace and rust brown or chestnut chest. Gray and white on the sides. Yellow bill. Orange legs and feet.

Female: brown duck with an orange and black bill and blue and white wing mark (speculum)

Juvenile: same as female, but with a yellow bill

Nest: ground; female builds; 1 brood per year

Eggs: 7-10; greenish to whitish, unmarked

Incubation: 26-30 days; female incubates

Fledging: 42-52 days; female leads young to food

Migration: partial to non-migrator in New Mexico

Food: seeds, plants, aquatic insects; will come to ground feeders offering corn

Compare: The male Northern Shoveler (pg. 289) has a white chest with rust on sides and a dark spoon-shaped bill. Breeding male Northern Pintail (pg. 175) has extremely long central tail feathers and a brown head.

Stan's Notes: A familiar duck of lakes and ponds, it's considered a type of dabbling duck, tipping forward in shallow water to feed on aquatic plants on the bottom. The name "Mallard" comes from the Latin *masculus*, meaning "male," referring to the habit of males not taking part in raising ducklings. Black central tail feathers of male curl upward. Both the male and female have white tails and white underwings. Returns to birthplace. Often associated with Mexican Mallard (see inset), which is very similar to the female Mallard.

female pg. 177

male

NORTHERN SHOVELER
Anas clypeata

YEAR-ROUND
MIGRATION
WINTER

Size: 20" (50 cm)

Male: Medium-sized duck with iridescent green head, rusty sides and white breast. Has an extraordinarily large spoon-shaped bill that is almost always held pointed toward water.

Female: same spoon-shaped bill, brown and black all over and blue wing patch

Juvenile: same as female

Nest: ground; female builds; 1 brood per year

Eggs: 9-12; olive without markings

Incubation: 22-25 days; female incubates

Fledging: 30-60 days; female leads young to food

Migration: complete migrator, to New Mexico, Mexico and Central America

Food: aquatic insects, plants

Compare: Similar to the male Mallard (pg. 287), but the male Northern Shoveler has a large, characteristic spoon-shaped bill.

Stan's Notes: One of several species of shoveler, so called because of the peculiar shape of its bill. The Northern Shoveler is the only species of these ducks in North America. Found in small flocks of 5-10, swimming low in water with its large bill pointed toward the water, as if it's too heavy to lift. Feeds mainly by filtering tiny aquatic insects and plants from the water's surface with its bill.

in flight

female pg. 309

male

COMMON MERGANSER
Mergus merganser

Size: 27" (69 cm)

YEAR-ROUND
WINTER

Male: Long, thin, duck-like bird with green head, a black back, and white sides, breast and neck. Has a long, pointed orange bill. Often appears to be black and white in poor light.

Female: same size and shape as the male, but with a rust red head, ragged "hair" on head, gray body with white chest and chin, and long, pointed orange bill

Juvenile: same as female

Nest: cavity; female lines old woodpecker cavity; 1 brood per year

Eggs: 9-11; ivory without markings

Incubation: 28-33 days; female incubates

Fledging: 70-80 days; female feeds young

Migration: complete migrator, to New Mexico, Mexico and Central America

Food: small fish, aquatic insects

Compare: Larger than male Mallard (pg. 287) and has a black back, bright white sides and a long pointed bill.

Stan's Notes: The merganser is a shallow water diver that feeds on small fish in 10-15 feet (3-4.5 m) of water. More commonly seen along rivers than lakes. The bill has a fine serrated-like edge to help catch slippery fish. Females often lay eggs in other merganser nests (egg dumping), resulting in broods of up to 15 young per mother. Male leaves the female when she starts to incubate eggs. Orphans are accepted by other merganser mothers with young.

male

female

MIGRATION

RUFOUS HUMMINGBIRD
Selasphorus rufus

Size: 3¾" (9.5 cm)

Male: Tiny burnt orange bird with a black throat patch (gorget) that reflects orange-red in sunlight. White chest. Green-to-tan flanks.

Female: same as male, but lacking the throat patch

Juvenile: similar to female

Nest: cup; female builds; 1-2 broods per year

Eggs: 1-3; white without markings

Incubation: 14-17 days; female incubates

Fledging: 21-26 days; female feeds young

Migration: complete, to Central and South America

Food: nectar, insects; will come to nectar feeders

Compare: Unique bird that is identified by the orange (rufous) coloring.

Stan's Notes: One of the smallest birds in the state. A bold, hardy hummer, it is often seen well out of its normal range in the western U.S., showing up along the East coast. Visits hummingbird feeders in your yard. Doesn't sing, but will chatter or buzz to communicate. Weighing 2-3 gm, it takes about five average-sized hummingbirds to equal the weight of one chickadee. Heart pumps an incredible 1,260 beats per minute. Male performs a spectacular pendulum-like flight over the perched female. After mating, female flies off to construct a nest and raise young, without any help from her mate. Constructs a soft, flexible nest that expands to accommodate the growing young. Doesn't nest in New Mexico.

female pg. 333

male

BULLOCK'S ORIOLE
Icterus bullockii

Size: 8" (20 cm)

Male: Bright orange and black bird. Black crown, eye line, nape, chin, wings and back with orange elsewhere. Bold white patch on the wings.

Female: dull yellow overall, pale white belly, white wing bars on gray-to-black wings

Juvenile: similar to female

Nest: pendulous; female and male build; 1 brood per year

Eggs: 4-6; pale white to gray, brown markings

Incubation: 12-14 days; female incubates

Fledging: 12-14 days; female and male feed young

Migration: complete, to Central and South America

Food: insects, berries, nectar; visits nectar feeders

Compare: A handsome bird. Look for male Bullock's bright orange and black markings, and the thin black line running through the eyes.

Stan's Notes: So closely related to Baltimore Orioles of the eastern U.S., at one time both were considered a single species. Interbreeds with Baltimores where their ranges overlap. Most common in the state where cottonwood trees grow along rivers and other wetlands. Also found at edges of clearings, in city parks, on farms and along irrigation ditches. Hanging sock-like nest is constructed of plant fibers such as inner bark of junipers and willows. Will incorporate yarn and thread into its nest if offered at the time of nest building.

female pg. 133

male

BLACK-HEADED GROSBEAK
Pheucticus melanocephalus

MIGRATION
SUMMER

Size: 8" (20 cm)

Male: Stocky bird with burnt orange chest, neck and rump. Black head, tail and wings with irregular-shaped white wing patches. Large bill with upper bill darker than lower.

Female: appears like a large sparrow, overall brown, lighter chest and belly, large two-toned bill, bold white eyebrows, yellow wing linings

Juvenile: similar to adult of the same sex

Nest: cup; female builds; 1 brood per year

Eggs: 3-4; pale green or bluish, brown markings

Incubation: 11-13 days; female and male incubate

Fledging: 11-13 days; female and male feed young

Migration: complete, to Mexico, Central America and South America

Food: seeds, insects, fruit; comes to seed feeders

Compare: Same size as the male Evening Grosbeak (pg. 331), but male Black-headed has an orange breast and lacks a yellow belly. Male Bullock's Oriole (pg. 295) has more white on the wings than the male Black-headed. Look for Black-headed's large bicolored bill.

Stan's Notes: A cosmopolitan bird that nests in a wide variety of habitats, seeming to prefer the foothills slightly more than other places. Both males and females sing and aggressively defend their nests against intruders. Song is very similar to the American Robin's and Western Tanager's, making it hard to tell them apart by song. Populations are increasing in New Mexico and across the U.S.

male

female pg. 89

yellow male

HOUSE FINCH
Carpodacus mexicanus

Size: 5" (13 cm)

Male: An orange red face, breast and rump, with a brown cap. Brown marking behind eyes. Brown wings streaked with white. A white belly with brown streaks.

Female: brown with a heavily streaked white chest

Juvenile: similar to female

Nest: cup, sometimes in cavities; female builds; 2 broods per year

Eggs: 4-5; pale blue, lightly marked

Incubation: 12-14 days; female incubates

Fledging: 15-19 days; female and male feed young

Migration: non-migrator to partial migrator; will move around to find food

Food: seeds, fruit, leaf buds; will visit seed feeders

Compare: Male Cassin's Finch (pg. 303) is similar, but is a rosy red unlike the orange red of male House Finch, and lacks a brown cap. Look for the streaked chest and belly, and brown cap of the male House Finch.

Stan's Notes: Very social bird. Visits feeders in small flocks. Likes nesting in hanging flower baskets. Incubating female fed by male. Loud, cheerful warbling song. Suffers a fatal eye disease that causes eyes to crust over. Historically it occurred from the Pacific coast to the Rocky Mountains, with a few reaching the eastern side. Birds introduced to Long Island, New York, in the 1940s have populated the entire eastern U.S. Now found all over the U.S. Rarely, some males are yellow (see inset) instead of red, probably due to poor diet.

female pg. 219

male

SUMMER

VERMILION FLYCATCHER
Pyrocephalus rubinus

Size: 6" (15 cm)

Male: A stunningly beautiful bird with a crimson red head, crest, chin, breast and belly. Black nape, back, wings and tail. Thick black line running through eyes. Thin black bill.

Female: gray head, neck and back, nearly white chin and breast, pink belly to undertail, black tail, thin black bill

Juvenile: similar to female, lacks a pink undertail

Nest: cup; female builds; 1-2 broods per year

Eggs: 2-4; white with brown markings

Incubation: 14-16 days; female and male incubate

Fledging: 14-16 days; female and male feed young

Migration: complete, to southern Arizona, throughout Mexico

Food: insects (mainly bees)

Compare: The unique bright crimson plumage with black wings make this bird easy to identify.

Stan's Notes: A uniquely colored flycatcher that is often found in open areas with shrubs and small trees close to water. Feeds mainly on insects, with bees making up a large part of its diet. Will perch on a thin branch, pumping tail up and down while waiting for an aerial insect. Flies out to snatch it, then returns to the perch. Drops to the ground for terrestrial insects. Male raises its crest, fluffs chest feathers, fans tail and sings a song during a fluttery flight to court females. Female builds a shallow nest of twigs and grasses and lines it with downy plant material. Male feeds female during incubation and brooding.

male

female pg. 111

CASSIN'S FINCH
Carpodacus cassinii

Size: 6½" (16 cm)

Male: Overall light wash of crimson red with an especially bright red crown. Distinct brown streaks on back and wings. White belly.

Female: overall brown to gray, fine black streaks on the back and wings, heavily streaked white chest and belly

Juvenile: similar to female

Nest: cup; female builds; 1-2 broods per year

Eggs: 3-5; white without markings

Incubation: 12-14 days; female incubates

Fledging: 14-18 days; female and male feed young

Migration: partial migrator to non-migrator; will move around to find food

Food: seeds, insects, fruits, berries; will visit seed feeders

Compare: Similar to the male House Finch (pg. 299), which has a brown cap, is heavily streaked on flanks and is orange red unlike the male Cassin's rosy red.

Stan's Notes: This is a mountain finch of coniferous forests. Usually forages for seeds on the ground, but eats evergreen buds and aspen and willow catkins. Breeds in May. A colony nester, depending on the regional source of food. The more food available, the larger the colony. Male sings a rapid warble, often imitating other birds such as jays, tanagers and grosbeaks. A cowbird host.

female pg. 327

male

RED CROSSBILL
Loxia curvirostra

YEAR-ROUND
WINTER

Size: 6½" (16 cm)

Male: Sparrow-sized bird, dirty red to orange with bright red crown and rump. Long, pointed, crossed bill. Dark brown wings and a short dark brown tail.

Female: pale yellow chest, light gray throat patch, a crossed bill, dark brown wings and tail

Juvenile: streaked with tinges of yellow, bill gradually crosses about 2 weeks after fledging

Nest: cup; female builds; 1 brood per year

Eggs: 3-4; bluish white with brown markings

Incubation: 14-18 days; female incubates

Fledging: 16-20 days; female and male feed young

Migration: non-migrator to irruptive migrator; moves around the state in winter to find food

Food: seeds, leaf buds; comes to seed feeders

Compare: Larger than the male House Finch (pg. 299) and has a unique crossed bill.

Stan's Notes: The long crossed bill is adapted for extracting seeds from pine and spruce cones, its favorite food. Often dangles upside down like a parrot to reach cones. Also seen on the ground where it eats grit, which helps digest food. Plumage can be highly variable among individuals. Nests in low elevation coniferous forests. While it is a resident nester, migrating crossbills from farther north move into the state in winter, searching for food, swelling populations. This irruptive behavior makes them common in some winters and scarce in others.

female pg. 167

male

REDHEAD
Aythya americana

YEAR-ROUND
WINTER

Size: 19" (48 cm)

Male: Rich red head and neck with a black breast and tail. Gray sides. Smoky gray wings and back. Tricolored bill with a light blue base, white ring and black tip.

Female: plain, soft brown duck with gray-to-white wing linings, top of head rounded, gray bill with black tip

Juvenile: similar to female

Nest: cup; female builds; 1 brood per year

Eggs: 9-14; pale white without markings

Incubation: 24-28 days; female and male incubate

Fledging: 56-73 days; female shows the young what to eat

Migration: complete migrator, to southwestern states, Mexico and Central America

Food: seeds, aquatic plants, insects

Compare: The male Northern Shoveler (pg. 289) has a green head and rusty sides unlike the male Redhead's gray sides.

Stan's Notes: A duck of permanent large bodies of water. Forages along the shoreline, feeding on seeds, aquatic plants and insects. Usually builds nest directly on surface of water, using large mats of vegetation. Female lays up to 75 percent of its eggs in the nests of other Redheads and several other duck species. Nests primarily in the Prairie Pothole region of the northern Great Plains. The overall populations seem to be increasing at about 2-3 percent each year.

in flight

male pg. 291

female

COMMON MERGANSER
Mergus merganser

Size: 27" (69 cm)

Female: A long, thin, duck-like bird with a rust red head and ragged "hair" on the back of head. Gray body with white chest and chin. Long, pointed orange bill.

Male: same size and shape as the female, but with a green head, black back, white sides and chest, and long, pointed orange bill

Juvenile: same as female

Nest: cavity; female lines old woodpecker cavity; 1 brood per year

Eggs: 9-11; ivory without markings

Incubation: 28-33 days; female incubates

Fledging: 70-80 days; female feeds young

Migration: complete migrator, to New Mexico, Mexico and Central America

Food: small fish, aquatic insects

Compare: Hard to confuse with other birds. Look for ragged "hair" on back of a red head, a long, pointed orange bill, white chest and chin.

Stan's Notes: Can be seen on just about any open water during the winter, but more common along rivers than lakes. The merganser is a shallow water diver that feeds on fish in 10-15 feet (3-4.5 m) of water. The bill has a fine serrated-like edge to help catch slippery fish. Females often lay their eggs in nests of other mergansers (egg dumping), resulting in broods of up to 15 young per mother. Male leaves the female as soon as she starts to incubate eggs. Orphans are accepted by other merganser mothers with young.

in flight

breeding

juvenile

winter

RING-BILLED GULL
Larus delawarensis

Size: 19" (48 cm); up to 4-foot wingspan

Male: A white bird with gray wings, black wing tips spotted with white, and a white tail, as seen in flight. Yellow bill with a black ring near tip. Yellowish legs and feet. Winter or non-breeding adult has a speckled brown back of head and nape of neck.

Female: same as male

Juvenile: mostly gray version of winter adult, has a dark band at end of tail

Nest: ground; female and male construct; 1 brood per year

Eggs: 2-4; off-white with brown markings

Incubation: 20-21 days; female and male incubate

Fledging: 20-40 days; female and male feed young

Migration: partial to complete, to New Mexico, Mexico

Food: insects, fish; scavenges for food

Compare: A large white gull with a black ring around the bill. One of the few gull species seen in New Mexico.

Stan's Notes: A common gull of garbage dumps and parking lots. It's expanding its range and remaining farther north longer during winter due to successful scavenging in cities. A three-year gull with a new, different plumage in each of the first three autumns. Attains ring on bill after its first winter and adult plumage in its third year. Defends a small area around nest. Doesn't nest in New Mexico.

in flight

SNOWY EGRET
Egretta thula

Size: 24" (60 cm); up to 3½-foot wingspan

Male: All-white bird. Black bill. Black legs. Bright yellow feet. Long feather plumes on head, neck and back during breeding season.

Female: same as male

Juvenile: similar to adult, but backs of legs are yellow

Nest: platform; female and male build; 1 brood per year

Eggs: 3-5; light blue-green without markings

Incubation: 20-24 days; female and male incubate

Fledging: 28-30 days; female and male feed young

Migration: complete, to Mexico

Food: aquatic insects, small fish

Compare: This is the only all-white egret in the state. Look for the long black legs and yellow feet to help identify.

Stan's Notes: Common in wetlands and often seen with other egrets. Colonies may include up to several hundred nests. Nests are low in shrubs 5-10 feet (1.5-3 m) tall or are on the ground, usually mixed among other egret and heron nests. Chicks hatch days apart (asynchronous), leading to starvation of last to hatch. Will actively "hunt" prey by moving around quickly, stirring up small fish and aquatic insects with its feet. In the breeding state, a yellow patch at the base of bill and the yellow feet turn orange-red. Was hunted to near extinction in the late 1800s for its feathers.

white
morph

blue morph

juvenile

Ross's Goose

in flight

SNOW GOOSE
Chen caerulescens

MIGRATION
WINTER

Size: 25-38" (63-96 cm); up to 4½-foot wingspan

Male: A mostly white goose with varying patches of black and brown. Black wing tips. Pink bill and legs. Some birds are grayish with a white head.

Female: same as male

Juvenile: overall dull gray with a dark bill

Nest: ground; female builds; 1 brood per year

Eggs: 3-5; white without markings

Incubation: 23-25 days; female incubates

Fledging: 45-49 days; female and male teach young to feed

Migration: complete, to parts of New Mexico, Arizona, California and Mexico

Food: aquatic insects and plants

Compare: Smaller than the Canada Goose (pg. 271), lacking a black neck and white chin strap.

Stan's Notes: Two color morphs. The more common white morph is pure white with black wing tips. Gray morph is often called blue, with a white head, gray chest and back, and pink bill and legs. Has a thick serrated bill for pulling up plants. Breeds in large colonies on the tundra of northern Canada. Females don't breed until they are 2-3 years old. Older females produce more eggs and are more successful than the younger females. Seen by the tens of thousands during migration and in the winter. Very similar to the Ross's Goose (see inset), which is slightly smaller in size and has a much smaller pink bill. Commonly seen with Ross's Geese and Sandhill Cranes.

male

female

YEAR-ROUND
SUMMER

LESSER GOLDFINCH
Carduelis psaltria

Size: 4½" (11 cm)

Male: Striking bright yellow underneath from the chin down to the base of tail. Black cap, tail and wings. Several white patches on wings. Greenish back.

Female: dull yellow underneath, lacks a black cap

Juvenile: same as female

Nest: cup; female builds; 1-2 broods per year

Eggs: 4-5; pale blue without markings

Incubation: 10-12 days; female incubates

Fledging: 12-14 days; female and male feed young

Migration: partial migrator to non-migrator; will move around the state to find food

Food: seeds, insects; will come to seed feeders

Compare: The male American Goldfinch (pg. 319) is slightly larger and has a yellow back unlike the greenish back of male Lesser Goldfinch. The female American Goldfinch (pg. 319) is larger and has darker wings than female Lesser Goldfinch.

Stan's Notes: The western males have greenish backs, while males in the eastern range (Texas) have entirely black heads and backs. Some females are extremely pale. Prefers forest edges or areas with short trees and a consistent water source. Unlike many birds, the Lesser Goldfinch's diet is about 96 percent seed, even in peak insect season. Will come to seed feeders. Late summer nesters, male feeds incubating female by regurgitating partially digested seeds. Pairs stay together all winter. Winter flocks can number in the hundreds.

winter male

male

female

AMERICAN GOLDFINCH
Carduelis tristis

Size: 5" (13 cm)

Male: A perky yellow bird with a black patch on forehead. Black tail with conspicuous white rump. Black wings with white wing bars. No marking on the chest. Dramatic change in color during winter, similar to female.

Female: dull olive yellow without a black forehead, with brown wings and a white rump

Juvenile: same as female

Nest: cup; female builds; 1 brood per year

Eggs: 4-6; pale blue without markings

Incubation: 10-12 days; female incubates

Fledging: 11-17 days; female and male feed young

Migration: partial migrator to complete; flocks of up to 20 move around North America

Food: seeds, insects; will come to seed feeders

Compare: The male Lesser Goldfinch (pg. 317) has a greenish back. The Pine Siskin (pg. 87) and female House Finch (pg. 89) have streaked breasts. Male Yellow Warbler (pg. 325) is all yellow with orange streaks on breast.

Stan's Notes: Most often found in open fields, scrubby areas and woodlands. Often called Wild Canary. A feeder bird that enjoys Nyger Thistle. Late summer nesting, uses the silky down from wild thistle for nest. Appears roller-coaster-like in flight. Listen for it to twitter in flight. Almost always in small flocks. This winter resident can be more common in some years and less common in others.

male

female

YEAR-ROUND
SUMMER

COMMON YELLOWTHROAT
Geothlypis trichas

Size: 5" (13 cm)

Male: Olive brown bird with bright yellow throat and breast, a white belly and a distinctive black mask outlined in white. A long, thin, pointed black bill.

Female: similar to male, lacks the black mask

Juvenile: same as female

Nest: cup; female builds; 2 broods per year

Eggs: 3-5; white with brown markings

Incubation: 11-12 days; female incubates

Fledging: 10-11 days; female and male feed young

Migration: complete, to Mexico and Central America

Food: insects

Compare: Found in a similar habitat as the American Goldfinch (pg. 319), but lacks the male's black forehead and wings. The male Yellow Warbler (pg. 325) has fine orange streaks on the breast and lacks male Yellowthroat's mask. Yellow-rumped Warbler (pg. 215) has only spots of yellow compared with the Yellowthroat's bright yellow breast.

Stan's Notes: A common warbler of open fields and marshes. Has a cheerful, well-known song, "witchity-witchity-witchity-witchity." The male performs a curious courtship display, bouncing in and out of tall grass while uttering an unusual song. The young remain dependent upon the parents longer than most warblers. A frequent cowbird host. Usually quiet and secretive during winter.

ORANGE-CROWNED WARBLER
Vermivora celata

Size: 5" (13 cm)

Male: An overall pale yellow bird with a dark line through eyes. Faint streaking on sides and chest. Small thin bill. Tawny orange crown, often invisible.

Female: same as male, but very slightly duller, often indistinguishable in the field

Juvenile: same as adults

Nest: cup; female builds; 1-2 broods per year

Eggs: 3-6; white with brown markings

Incubation: 12-14 days; female incubates

Fledging: 8-10 days; female and male feed young

Migration: complete, to Mexico and Central America

Food: insects, fruit, nectar

Compare: Yellow Warbler (pg. 325) is brighter yellow with orange streaking on the male's breast. Male Common Yellowthroat (pg. 321) has a very distinctive black mask.

Stan's Notes: A widespread warbler and nester in the state, but is frequently seen more during migration when large groups move together. Builds a bulky, well-concealed cup nest on the ground with the nest rim at ground level. Known to feed at sapsucker taps and drink flower nectar. The orange crown tends to be hidden and is rarely seen in the field. A widespread breeder, from western Texas to Alaska and across Canada.

male

female

YELLOW WARBLER
Dendroica petechia

Size: 5" (13 cm)

Male: Yellow warbler with orange streaks on the chest and belly. Long, pointed dark bill.

Female: same as male, but lacking orange streaking

Juvenile: similar to female, only much duller

Nest: cup; female builds; 1 brood per year

Eggs: 4-5; white with brown markings

Incubation: 11-12 days; female incubates

Fledging: 10-12 days; female and male feed young

Migration: complete, to Mexico, Central America and South America

Food: insects

Compare: Look for orange streaking on chest of male. Orange-crowned Warbler (pg. 323) is paler yellow. Male American Goldfinch (pg. 319) has black wings and forehead. The female Yellow Warbler is similar to the female American Goldfinch (pg. 319), but lacks white wing bars.

Stan's Notes: A widespread and common warbler in New Mexico, seen in gardens and shrubby areas near water. It is a prolific insect eater, gleaning small caterpillars and other insects from tree leaves. Male is often seen higher up in trees than the female. Female is less conspicuous. Starts to migrate in August and returns in late April. Males arrive 1-2 weeks before females to claim territories. Migrates at night in mixed flocks of warblers. Rests and feeds days.

female

male pg. 305

RED CROSSBILL
Loxia curvirostra

Size: 6½" (16 cm)

Female: A pale yellow-gray sparrow-sized bird with a pale yellow chest and light gray patch on the throat. Long, pointed, crossed bill. Dark brown wings and a short dark brown tail.

Male: dirty red to orange with a bright red crown and rump, a crossed bill, dark brown wings and a short dark brown tail

Juvenile: streaked with tinges of yellow, bill gradually crosses about 2 weeks after fledging

Nest: cup; female builds; 1 brood per year

Eggs: 3-4; bluish white with brown markings

Incubation: 14-18 days; female incubates

Fledging: 16-20 days; female and male feed young

Migration: non-migrator to irruptive migrator; moves around the state in winter to find food

Food: seeds, leaf buds; comes to seed feeders

Compare: Larger than the female American Goldfinch (pg. 319). Look for the unique crossed bill.

Stan's Notes: The long crossed bill is adapted for extracting seeds from pine and spruce cones, its favorite food. Often dangles upside down like a parrot to reach cones. Also seen on the ground where it eats grit, which helps digest food. Plumage can be highly variable among individuals. Nests in low elevation coniferous forests. While it is a resident nester, migrating crossbills from farther north move into the state in winter, searching for food, swelling populations. This irruptive behavior makes them common in some winters and scarce in others.

non-breeding male

male

female

MIGRATION
SUMMER

WESTERN TANAGER
Piranga ludoviciana

Size: 7¼" (18.5 cm)

Male: A canary yellow bird with a red head. Black back, tail, wings. One white and one yellow wing bar. Non-breeding lacks the red head.

Female: duller than male, lacking the red head

Juvenile: similar to female

Nest: cup; female builds; 1 brood per year

Eggs: 3-5; light blue with brown markings

Incubation: 11-13 days; female incubates

Fledging: 13-15 days; female and male feed young

Migration: complete, to Mexico and Central America

Food: insects, fruit

Compare: Male American Goldfinch (pg. 319) has a black forehead and lacks the breeding male Tanager's red head. Unique combination of colors makes the male hard to misidentify. Female Bullock's Oriole (pg. 333) lacks the female Tanager's single yellow wing bars.

Stan's Notes: Common throughout most of New Mexico. Male is stunning in its breeding plumage. Feeds mainly on insects such as bees, wasps, grasshoppers and cicadas. Feeds to a lesser degree on fruit. Male feeds female as she incubates. Female builds a cup nest in a horizontal fork of a coniferous tree, well away from the main trunk, from 20-40 feet (6-12 m) above ground. This is the farthest nesting tanager species, reaching up into the Northwest Territories of Canada. An early autumn migrant, often seen migrating in late July (when non-breeding males lack red heads). Can be seen in just about any habitat during migration.

male

juvenile

female

EVENING GROSBEAK
Coccothraustes vespertinus

YEAR-ROUND

Size: 8" (20 cm)

Male: A striking bird with a stocky body, a large ivory-to-greenish bill and bright yellow eyebrows. Dirty yellow head, black-and-white wings and tail and yellow rump and belly.

Female: similar to male, with softer colors and a gray head and throat

Juvenile: similar to female, with a brown bill

Nest: cup; female builds; 1 brood per year

Eggs: 3-4; blue with brown markings

Incubation: 12-14 days; female incubates

Fledging: 13-14 days; female and male feed young

Migration: non-migrator to irruptive; moves around in winter to find food

Food: seeds, insects, fruit; comes to seed feeders

Compare: Larger than its close relative, the American Goldfinch (pg. 319). Look for the dark head, bright yellow eyebrows and large thick bill of the male Evening Grosbeak.

Stan's Notes: One of the largest finches. Characteristic undulating finch-like flight. An unusually large bill for cracking seeds, its main food source. Often seen on gravel roads eating gravel, from which it gets minerals, salt and grit to grind the seeds it eats. A year-round resident, it is more obvious during winter because it moves in large flocks, searching for food, often coming to feeders. Sheds the outer layer of its bill in spring, exposing a blue green bill.

male pg. 295

female

BULLOCK'S ORIOLE
Icterus bullockii

Size: 8" (20 cm)

Female: Dull yellow head and chest. Gray-to-black wings with white wing bars. A pale white belly. Gray back, as seen in flight.

Male: bright orange and black, bold white patch on wings

Juvenile: similar to female

Nest: pendulous; female and male build; 1 brood per year

Eggs: 4-6; pale white to gray, brown markings

Incubation: 12-14 days; female incubates

Fledging: 12-14 days; female and male feed young

Migration: complete, to Central and South America

Food: insects, berries, nectar; visits nectar feeders

Compare: Female Scott's Oriole (pg. 335) is larger and lacks the pale white belly. Female Western Tanager (pg. 329) has a black back unlike the female Oriole's gray back. Look for the overall dull yellow and gray appearance of the female Bullock's Oriole.

Stan's Notes: So closely related to Baltimore Orioles of the eastern U.S., at one time both were considered a single species. Interbreeds with Baltimores where their ranges overlap. Most common in the state where cottonwood trees grow along rivers and other wetlands. Also found at edges of clearings, in city parks, on farms and along irrigation ditches. Hanging sock-like nest is constructed of plant fibers such as inner bark of junipers and willows. Will incorporate yarn and thread into its nest if offered at the time of nest building.

male

female

SCOTT'S ORIOLE
Icterus parisorum

Size: 9" (22.5 cm)

Male: A black head, neck, back, upper breast and tail with lemon yellow belly, shoulders and rump. Long, pointed, slightly down-curved black bill. Dark eyes. Two white wing bars.

Female: similar to male, but has much less black

Juvenile: grayer than female, yellow under belly only

Nest: pendulous; female builds; 1-2 broods a year

Eggs: 2-4; pale blue with brown markings

Incubation: 14-16 days; female and male incubate

Fledging: 14-16 days; female and male feed young

Migration: complete, to Mexico

Food: insects, fruit, nectar; will come to orange or grapefruit halves and nectar feeders

Compare: The female Bullock's Oriole (pg. 333) has a pale white belly. Male American Goldfinch (pg. 319) is much smaller and has black on the forehead, not the entire head.

Stan's Notes: Found in open dry areas often associated with yucca and palm. Like other oriole species, female constructs a sock-like pouch that hangs from the end of a thin branch or is woven into a hole in a palm leaf. Populations have increased over the past 100 years due to planting of palm trees. Male is yellow, not orange, like other male orioles. Hunts by gleaning insects and caterpillars from leaves. Uses its long pointed bill to poke holes in bases of flowers to get nectar. Parents feed their young by regurgitating a mixture of insects and fruit. Named after General Winfield Scott, who fought in the Mexican War.

WESTERN KINGBIRD
Tyrannus verticalis

Size: 9" (22.5 cm)

Male: Bright yellow belly and yellow under wings. Gray head and chest, often with white chin. Wings and tail are dark gray to nearly black with white outer edges on tail.

Female: same as male

Juvenile: similar to adult, less yellow and more gray

Nest: cup; female and male construct; 1 brood per year

Eggs: 3-4; white with brown markings

Incubation: 18-20 days; female incubates

Fledging: 16-18 days; female and male feed young

Migration: complete, to Central America

Food: insects, berries

Compare: The Eastern Kingbird (pg. 231) lacks any yellow of the Western Kingbird. Western Meadowlark (pg. 339) shares the Western Kingbird's yellow belly, but has a distinctive black V-shaped necklace.

Stan's Notes: A bird of open country, frequently seen sitting on top of the same shrub or fence post. Hunts by watching for crickets, bees, grasshoppers and other insects and flying out to catch them, then returns to perch. Parents teach young how to hunt, bringing wounded insects back to the nest for the young to chase. Returns in March. Builds nest right away, often in the fork of a small single trunk tree. Common throughout the state, nesting in trees around homesteads and farms. Some may winter in southern New Mexico.

WESTERN MEADOWLARK
Sturnella neglecta

Size: 9" (22.5 cm)

Male: Heavy-bodied bird with a short tail. Brown back, yellow chest and prominent black V-shaped necklace. White outer tail feathers.

Female: same as male

Juvenile: same as adult

Nest: cup, on the ground in dense cover; female builds; 1-2 broods per year

Eggs: 3-5; white with brown markings

Incubation: 13-15 days; female incubates

Fledging: 11-13 days; female and male feed young

Migration: non-migrator to partial migrator

Food: insects, seeds

Compare: Western Kingbird (pg. 337) shares a yellow belly, but lacks the Meadowlark's distinctive black V-shaped necklace.

Stan's Notes: This bird is most common in open country. Named "Meadowlark" because it's a bird of meadows and sings like larks of Europe. Best known for its wonderful song. Not a member of the lark family, it belongs to the blackbird family. Related to blackbirds such as grackles and orioles. Like other blackbird family members, it catches prey by poking its long thin bill into places such as holes in the ground or in tufts of grass, where bugs are hiding. Opening its mouth to create space, the bird extracts insects. Often perches on fence posts. Quickly dives into tall grass when approached. Seen throughout New Mexico, while the Eastern Meadowlark occurs in eastern areas of the state (map reflects the combined range). Nearly identical in appearance, but they sing distinctly different songs.

HELPFUL RESOURCES

Birder's Bug Book, The. Waldbauer, Gilbert. Cambridge: Harvard University Press, 1998.

Birder's Dictionary. Cox, Randall T. Helena, MT: Falcon Press Publishing, 1996.

Birder's Handbook, The. Ehrlich, Paul R., David S. Dobkin and Darryl Wheye. New York: Simon and Schuster, 1988.

Birds Do It, Too: The Amazing Sex Life of Birds. Harrison, Kit and George H. Harrison. Minocqua, WI: Willow Creek Press, 1997.

Birds of Forest, Yard, and Thicket. Eastman, John. Mechanicsburg, PA: Stackpole Books, 1997.

Birds of North America. Kaufman, Kenn. New York: Houghton Mifflin, 2000.

Blackbirds of the Americas. Orians, Gordon H. Seattle: University of Washington Press, 1985.

Cry of the Sandhill Crane, The. Grooms, Steve. Minocqua, WI: NorthWord Press, 1992.

Dictionary of American Bird Names, The. Choate, Ernest A. Boston: Harvard Common Press, 1985.

Everything You Never Learned About Birds. Rupp, Rebecca. Pownal, VT: Storey Publishing, 1997.

Field Guide to the Birds of North America: Third Edition. Washington, DC: National Geographic Society, 1999.

Field Guide to Warblers of North America, A. Dunn, Jon and Kimball Garrett. Boston: Houghton Mifflin, 1997.

Field Guide to Western Birds, A. Peterson, Roger Tory. Boston: Houghton Mifflin, 1998.

Folklore of Birds. Martin, Laura C. Old Saybrook, CT: Globe Pequot Press, 1996.

Guide to Bird Behavior, A: Vol I, II, III. Stokes, Donald and Lillian Stokes. Boston: Little, Brown and Company, 1989.

How Birds Migrate. Kerlinger, Paul. Mechanicsburg, PA: Stackpole Books, 1995.

Lives of Birds, The: Birds of the World and Their Behavior. Short, Lester L. Collingdale, PA: DIANE Publishing, 2000.

Lives of North American Birds. Kaufman, Kenn. Boston: Houghton Mifflin, 1996.

Living on the Wind. Weidensaul, Scott. New York: North Point Press, 2000.

National Audubon Society: North American Birdfeeder Handbook. Burton, Robert. New York: Dorling Kindersley Publishing, 1995.

National Audubon Society: The Sibley Guide to Bird Life and Behavior. Edited by David Allen Sibley, Chris Elphick and John B. Dunning, Jr. New York: Alfred A. Knopf, 2001.

National Audubon Society: The Sibley Guide to Birds. Sibley, David Allen. New York: Alfred A. Knopf, 2000.

Photographic Guide to North American Raptors, A. Wheeler, Brian K. and William S. Clark. New York: Academic Press, 1999.

Raptors of Western North America: The Wheeler Guides. Wheeler, Brian K. Princeton, NJ: Princeton University Press, 2003.

Secret Lives of Birds, The. Gingras, Pierre. Toronto: Key Porter Books, 1997.

Secrets of the Nest. Dunning, Joan. Boston: Houghton Mifflin, 1994.

Sparrows and Buntings: A Guide to the Sparrows and Buntings of North America and the World. Byers, Clive, Jon Curson and Urban Olsson. New York: Houghton Mifflin, 1995.

Stokes Bluebird Book: The Complete Guide to Attracting Bluebirds. Stokes, Donald and Lillian Stokes. Boston: Little, Brown and Company, 1991.

Stokes Field Guide to Birds: Western Region. Stokes, Donald and Lillian Stokes. Boston: Little, Brown and Company, 1996.

New Mexico Birding Hotline

To report unusual bird sightings or possibly hear recordings of where birds have been seen, you can often call pre-recorded hotlines detailing such information. Since these hotlines are usually staffed by volunteers, and phone numbers and even the organizations that host them often change, the phone numbers are not listed here. To obtain the numbers, go to your favorite internet search engine, type in something like "rare bird alert hotline New Mexico" and follow the links provided.

Web Pages

The internet is a valuable place to learn more about birds. You may find birding on the net a fun way to discover additional information or to spend a long winter night. These web sites will assist you in your pursuit of birds. If a web address doesn't work (they often change a bit), just enter the name of the group into a search engine to track down the new web address.

Site	Address
New Mexico Ornithological Society	http://mvar.nmsu.edu/nmos/index.html
New Mexico Birding	www.interaktv.com/NM/NMBirding.html
American Birding Association	www.americanbirding.org
Cornell Lab of Ornithology	www.birds.cornell.edu
Author Stan Tekiela's home page	www.naturesmart.com

ABOUT THE AUTHOR

Stan Tekiela is a naturalist, author and wildlife photographer with a Bachelor of Science degree in Natural History from the University of Minnesota. He has been a professional naturalist for more than 20 years and is a member of the Minnesota Naturalist Association, Minnesota Ornithologist Union, Outdoor Writers Association of America and Canon Professional Services. Stan actively studies and photographs birds throughout the U.S. He received an Excellence in Interpretation award from the National Association for Interpretation, and a regional award for Commitment to Outdoor Education. A columnist and radio personality, his syndicated column appears in over 20 cities and he can be heard on a number of radio stations. Stan resides in Victoria, Minnesota, with wife Katherine and daughter Abigail. He can be contacted via his web page at www.naturesmart.com.

Stan authors several field guides for other states including guides for birds, birds of prey, reptiles and amphibians, wildflowers and trees.